The Highland Year

THE HIGHLAND YEAR

A Sketchbook of the Open Road

ALEXANDER MAITLAND

Methuen . London

First published in Great Britain 1988
by Methuen London Ltd
11 New Fetter Lane, London EC4P 4EE
© 1988 Alexander Maitland

Typeset by Wyvern Typesetting Ltd, Bristol
Origination by Reprocolor Llovet S.A., Barcelona
Printed and bound in Spain by
Cayfosa Industria Grafica, Barcelona

British Library Cataloguing in Publication Data

Maitland, Alexander
    The Highland year: a sketchbook of the open road.
    1. Highlands (Scotland) – Description and travel
    I. Title
    914.11'104858   DA880.H7

    ISBN 0-413-15130-1

To my mother and father

Acknowledgements

I wish to thank the editors of *The Scotsman*, *Country Life* and *The Field* for their kind permission to quote from, or present in a revised form, articles which have appeared in their various papers over the years. I should also like to thank Macmillan London Ltd for permission to reproduce the quote on page 184 from Seton Gordon's *Highways and Byways in the West Highlands* (1935; 1979).

Throughout the weeks spent tramping in Perthshire and Argyllshire, my parents helped and encouraged me in every way imaginable. I cannot thank them sufficiently. My wife, Margaret, made valuable suggestions and carefully arranged and identified my small collection of wildflowers.

From Deeside, and latterly from Inverness-shire, John and Audrey Harrower have encouraged my efforts as an artist; I have been privileged to share their annual Highland exhibitions since 1980.

Thanks to Sebastian Guly, who entertained me at Sligachan on the Isle of Skye, I was able to renew my acquaintance with the cottage where several happy winters were spent in the late 1960s. The owner of the cottage, Mrs R.C. Wakefield, made us welcome when we first arrived there and introduced us to many kind friends whose company added much to our enjoyment of the island.

I owe much besides to the good people I met casually along the way: landowners, gamekeepers and shepherds, fishermen, shopkeepers and many others who spared the time to talk to me or offer a few words of helpful advice.

I wish also to thank the Librarian and staff of The Royal Geographical Society who helped me to find books and answered numerous enquiries.

For anyone interested, the pencil and watercolour drawings which illustrate this book were made on 185gm and 300gm Arches papers, which I have found to be very satisfactory.

Alexander Maitland
London 1988

December

A rosy flush lingering at the western horizon over Skye shone in the calm, gently rippling waters of the Inner Sound. The Cuillin Hills stood out sharp and clear in dark-blue silhouette, here and there tinged with streaks of coral-pink and crimson. Their deep blue shadow hovered on the water where the lights of Kyleakin harbour reflected like shimmering yellow rods, each one tipped with a golden star.

As I sat in my car at the head of the concrete slipway, admiring the sunset, three of the rods slowly detached themselves from the rest and through the open window I heard the faint, grinding churn of the ferry as it began its short crossing to the mainland.

The rose-pink sky and the rose-pink sea and the cold, salty smack of sea air brought back a host of vivid memories. I had not been near Skye for fifteen years. It was longer still since I had first arrived on the island to spend the winter at Sligachan, writing a book. It felt marvellous to be going there again and yet, for all sorts of reasons, the good feeling was clouded with apprehension. I had no idea what I might find, or how much would have altered during the interval. I wondered how easy or how difficult it would be to pick up old friendships where they had left off. Nobody was expecting me, for the journey north had been arranged, as usual, at the last minute, with few preparations. It occurred to me that perhaps this was just as well.

My life had changed too, in various ways. When I first visited Skye in 1966, I had been little more than a boy. Many of the people I had known then had been older than I was now. It was hard to imagine them – men and women I had tramped and climbed with, and with whom I had sat up talking into the small hours on a stormy night. I thought, My God, we will probably not even recognise one another after so long.…

A fair-haired boy clad in a thick polo-neck jersey and yellow oilskins banged his fist on the car roof.

'That'll be two pounds forty-three,' he demanded, and in exchange he gave me a torn-off receipt. The price of the fare seemed to me ridiculously exact. 'Why two pounds forty-three?' I chaffed him. 'Why don't they make it a round two pounds fifty?'

The boy shrugged as he delved into his hard leather satchel for the change. 'Somebody somewhere has worked it out,' he replied. 'That's the winter rate, you see. In the summer, it's two pounds forty-six.'

Eccentricities of this kind are very common in the Highlands, just as the most ordinary-seeming people one meets can be full of surprises.

The previous night I had stayed in a bungalow near Spean Bridge, where the owners did bed and breakfast. The bungalow was sparsely furnished, without much character, but it was warm and clean and perfectly adequate.

The owners, Tony and Madge, had moved to Inverness-shire from a small town in Lancashire. They had sold their newsagents business on impulse and headed north in their Dormobile in search of a new and better life. They were in their late fifties and had no regrets.

Tony was bald, with a round oblong body and very thin short legs. He looked exactly like a boiled egg perched in an egg-cup. Madge had bunions and shuffled about in loose-fitting brown sandals. She ran the bed and breakfast business and was much more assertive than her husband.

'We were up at five every morning,' she told me, shaking her head solemnly for emphasis. 'It were a six-day week. Not like some office job, you understand. We'd get the papers sorted by six-thirty for the delivery boys and we never closed t'shop before seven at night. Same on Saturdays. I tell you straight, folks wouldn't stand for it nowadays.'

When I asked what had brought them to such a quiet, out-of-the-way place, Tony giggled. 'That were pure accident. To this day, nobody will believe it. We got right up as far as Inverness and I went into a shop and bought the evening paper. There was a big house advertised in the Shetlands and we both thought it sounded all right. But when we worked it out, it would have cost us near two hundred pounds just to go and look at it. If we'd not liked the house, it'd have been all that good money wasted.

'There was another house for sale at Fort William, quite a big place with five or six bedrooms, but it had gone by the time we rang the solicitors. Any road, the solicitor told us about this place and we came straight down and had a look.' By this time, Tony was giggling uncontrollably. 'House were just a shell, you see. It had no roof and no windows either. Some local chap had started to build it on his own like, and then he ran out of cash. The garden, if you could call it a garden, was like a jungle. But I saw that the place had potential, so we decided to give it a go. I bought a second-hand caravan and we lived in that till the work was finished and then we sold the caravan and moved into the house. God, it were hard work! And it cost me a good few bob by the time it were done, I can tell you. What a carry on! It were like they say on television, a true-life adventure.'

'If you hadn't found the house, would you have kept on looking?' I asked.

Madge interrupted. 'That's hard to say. Maybe we'd have turned and gone back south. We might have tried the Yorkshire dales. My folks came from Yorkshire originally. But I like being near to mountains. I think that them as climbs them are born lunatics, mind you. But I enjoy looking at mountains from a distance. Tony's the same. We'd not have wanted to live in a town again, that's for sure.'

Madge had started her bed and breakfasts as soon as the bungalow had been decorated. Tony had done most of this work himself and he was tremendously proud of the oil-fired central heating system which he had installed, again entirely on his own. 'Tony's right good with his hands,' said Madge. 'There's not much he won't tackle. Tony's a worker and so am I. Our neighbours sometimes bring me clothes that need altering. I tell them what I think it's going to cost, but in the end they usually pay me whatever they feel like. They're a funny crowd really. Quite different to what we've been used to. But it works out easier that way. Keeps everybody happy.'

In many ways Tony and Madge's lives were as spartan as their bungalow. I noticed from their conversation how much making money mattered to them. Since settling in Inverness-shire, they had managed, for the first time in their lives, to save enough to go abroad every year on holiday. They said they liked Germany best, and they had been on several wine-tasting cruises on the Rhine.

Even so, they assured me that they were both virtually teetotallers. Drinking, I discovered, meant beer or spirits. Apparently wine did not count. Madge showed me her enormous collection of coloured picture-postcards, and there was a cuckoo clock, made to look like a Tyrolean ski-chalet, in the front parlour. Every alternate hour, after the 'cuckoo', the clock played 'Edelweiss' or 'Lara's Theme' from *Doctor Zhivago*.

While I sat drinking a pot of tea and writing up my notes, Tony and Madge ate their supper and watched 'Coronation Street' in the kitchen across the hall. I felt as if I were in Crewe or Birmingham.

The bungalow's atmosphere had almost nothing to do with the Highlands. It seemed like a tiny outpost isolated from its surroundings. There were German wood carvings ranged along the sideboard, interspersed with gaudy painted German beer mugs. There were framed photographs of Mainz and Koblenz hanging on the walls. As I wrote, Tony and Madge's arthritic Alsatian, Helga, lay panting on the carpet beside me. The thermometer by the door, a particularly hideous souvenir from their last package tour, registered eighty degrees. The air in the room was dry and oppressive and smelled heavily of dog.

I got up and drew the curtains and looked outside. The ground was white with frost and a lochan further down the glen shone white and glassy beneath the full moon and the sky filled with stars. I felt suddenly alienated from everything I had come to rediscover.

The cuckoo's hatch clicked open, the clock chimed the hour and a metallic chorus of 'Edelweiss' followed. The melody was accurate and immediately recognisable, but totally expressionless.

Madge poked her head round the door. 'No need to hurry in the morning,' she said. 'You'll get a proper breakfast. Cereal and then sausage, egg and bacon. All the trimmings. There's toast and marmalade after that and tea or coffee, whichever you prefer. We believe in doing things right in this house. Just like they do in Germany.'

The cottage where I lived for five winters stands close to the Allt Dearg burn, at the foot of the Black Cuillins.

The jagged peaks of Sgùrr nan Gillean, the Basteir Tooth and the gentler Bruach na Frìthe give an impression of being pinned to the sky, their slate-grey rumpled fabric falling in deep folds to the brown moorland below. Faint tracks across the moor bordering Glen Varagill show the route taken by James Boswell and Dr Samuel Johnson during their celebrated tour of the Hebrides in 1773. For more than a century, the rivers flowing through Glen Varagill and Glen Sligachan have been popular with trout and salmon fishermen; but it is mountaineering above all that put Sligachan on the map. Generations of artists, writers and photographers have drawn inspiration from the magnificent scenery – among them

William Daniell, Seton Gordon and W.A. Poucher. The area itself is not particularly large, but it is one of the most interesting I know.

From Sconser I drove to Sligachan, where friends told me that the Cuillin cottage had been let for the past two months; the tenant, they said, had gone. The owner of the cottage, to my great disappointment, was also away. However, my friends at the hotel assured me that there could be no harm whatever in going up to the place, which had been my home, after all, for several years. And so I drove up and parked the car at the road-end, half a mile from the cottage, and settled down to sketch the great shale-covered cone of Glamaig.

The ground was frozen hard. A bitter cold wind swept down from the stark fortress of hills, its passage unmarked by the tangled, frosted grass and heather. Glamaig and Marsco were half-obscured by clouds and flecked with snow which lay in patches on the low ground. The rough track leading to the cottage was dotted with puddles which the hard frost of the previous night had turned to solid sheets of ice. The sky between the clouds shone like tempered steel. The wind on my face was sharp and cutting like a knife.

I had been sitting there for perhaps twenty minutes when to my surprise the cottage door opened, and a tall figure emerged carrying a bucket in each hand and hurried down to the burn.

So the cottage had not been deserted, after all. I knew that the man must have seen my car and for a moment I felt sorry. I remembered only too well how I had longed for company on many a winter's night, when the rain lashed at the cottage windows and the wind moaned and thundered in the chimney. And yet, when the first hill walkers appeared at the end of the track in spring, I knew how much I had resented their presence in this beautiful, wild landscape whose emptiness I had got accustomed to.

I had been told that the tenant was a writer, something of a recluse, and it seemed unfair to intrude upon his privacy. But after a while longer, I thought – why not? – and I packed up my sketchbook and colours. It was bitterly cold; hardly the weather for sitting about out of doors. Besides, my curiosity had by then been sufficiently aroused to banish any finer feelings.

Through the kitchen window I saw the recluse standing at a table under a naked bulb, ladling water from one of the buckets into a kettle. The table was littered with pots and pans, jugs, receptacles of all sorts, all brim-full of water. When I knocked at the front door, which stood slightly ajar, the man glanced up and grinned.

'Come in,' he said. 'Sorry about this mess. The electric pump's gone on the blink again and I've spent the whole morning getting water up from the burn.'

He stood about six foot three in his stockinged feet, and was powerfully built with large hands and feet and a shock of wavy brown hair. I guessed he was in his early thirties. His huge presence seemed to fill the room entirely, and I was reminded of someone whom Edith Sitwell once described, who always appeared to be in three or four places at the same time.

The recluse grinned again. 'You look absolutely perished. May I offer you a cup of coffee, or perhaps you'd rather have tea? Don't worry about getting in the way. I was just about to brew up anyhow.' We introduced ourselves and I made the usual insincere apologies for arriving without warning, which the recluse, whose name was Sebastian, accepted and immediately brushed aside. We carried our mugs of coffee into the sitting-room and sat down in front of the empty hearth. I shivered instinctively and held the coffee mug in both hands to get warm.

The room was very much as I remembered it. The same broken-down sofa and comfortable armchairs. The little sun-bleached mahogany table with one short leg, where I had worked hard for months, writing a life of the Nile explorer, Speke. The faded, tartan curtains and the same black and white photographs of the Cuillins, with the names of the peaks written above them in Indian ink, hanging on the white vee-boarded walls. I had kept the room tidy, being a naturally – or as my wife would say – neurotically tidy individual. But now the floor was strewn with open suitcases and various odds and ends of clothing: socks, mufflers, climbing boots and a pair of old torn trousers which had been pulled off and left lying, half inside-out, in a corner. Judging by the musty smell and the little heap of damp caked ashes in the grate, a fire had not been lit in the room for some considerable time.

Sebastian appeared to read my thoughts. 'I don't bother much with fires,' he remarked. 'Haven't really felt the need. We've had an awful lot of rain during the past month and up to now the weather has been pretty mild. Anyhow, I'm usually out walking or climbing and in the evenings I have a meal and go to bed early. I don't seem to feel the cold like some people.'

I found Sebastian very easy to talk to and our conversation flowed on naturally. I told him about my connection with the cottage and when I had lived there and what I had been doing. I added, 'They say that you're a writer too.'

Sebastian made a silly face. 'Oh, look here, that's a bit of an exaggeration.' And as he spoke, he coloured slightly. 'It's true I've been trying to write. But apart from a few scraps of pretty awful poetry – I suppose I ought to call it verse – I haven't much to show for it.'

He reached over his shoulder for a pipe and matches that lay behind him on the writing table, while I lit a cigarette. Then we talked for a while about the mountains and the weather and what Sebastian had been doing since he arrived there, and what he had been doing before that.

'I badly needed to be on my own,' he said, screwing up his eyes as he relit his pipe. 'Truth is, I've been in a bit of a quandary: what to do next and so on. I walked past the cottage a year or two ago and it seemed like a good place to sit quietly and think in.'

Sebastian explained that, after leaving Oxford, he had decided to become a Roman Catholic priest. By then he had spent a year in a seminary, a well-known diocesan establishment in Chelsea, not far from where we live.

'The problem is,' he went on, 'I feel more and more strongly that a priest doesn't have to be celibate to do a good job. The idea of being married and having a normal sort of life is very important to me. The idea of shutting oneself away from the world – being a Trappist monk or a nun, for example – doesn't make any sense. The self-discipline, including subduing the cravings of the flesh, as they say, isn't easy; but then I don't believe you're doing anybody else much good either.'

'Can't you somehow manage to combine the two?' I asked. 'I mean, live as a good Catholic and get involved with some sort of community work. After all, you needn't be a priest to achieve that.'

Sebastian nodded and said he had thought of this alternative. Perhaps it was the right thing for him after all. He had already

worked for a year in a hospice in London's East End, where in spite of chronic overcrowding, lack of amenities and joblessness, the folk living in Sebastian's neighbourhood clung together. 'It's true,' he remarked, 'there were some really bad characters among them, but you'll find those anywhere. Most of the people I met were decent and eager to work. They were a bit rough around the edges, but they were good-hearted as well. I loved the West Indians. They've a wonderful charisma and a wonderful sense of humour. Nearly always smiling.'

'That's something you notice right away up here,' I said. 'Hardly any coloured people at all. It makes quite a change after London.'

In Skye, there had been, and probably still was, a good deal of colour prejudice, but in fairness I think no more or less than you might expect to find in other equally remote parts of the country. I told Sebastian about an Indian, called Patel, who ran a mobile shop in Skye in the 'sixties. To start with Mr Patel found the locals impossible to understand; but he was good-natured and polite and provided a useful service, and as a result he achieved a certain amount of popularity. One of the crofters told me how Mr Patel sometimes dropped in at the village pub for a glass of lemonade during his delivery round. My informant sighed: 'Silly wee man, he'd come waddling in, all smiles, and somebody would say, "How are you today, Mr To-Hell?" and he would say, "Oh, I am fine today thanks and how are you?" Patel or To-Hell, he didn't seem to know the difference.'

As a matter of fact, Mr Patel had an honours degree in commercial studies from Bombay, whereas I doubt very much that the crofter who poked fun at him was capable of writing his own name.

'It has been tremendously important to me to get away and think things through,' said Sebastian, 'but I mustn't stay on Skye too long. I feel I'm getting to the stage where I'm wasting time. The trouble is, I'm lazy. I hate having to make decisions. Take something as simple as reading. I have to force myself to pick up a book and read it to the end.'

On the table beside him, I had noticed paperback editions of *War and Peace* and *Les Misérables*.

'If I ever got down to writing a novel,' said Sebastian, 'it would be on the same epic scale as Tolstoy. Hundreds and hundreds of pages telling the stories of men and women and their families over successive generations. But I don't suppose I'll ever get started, or, if I get started, have the drive to finish it. I suppose you must find this hard to understand.'

I told him about writing my first book, a biography of John Hanning Speke, who discovered the source of the White Nile. Much of the research had involved breaking new ground, collecting letters, reports and so on which had been gathering dust for a century or more in West Country attics and public libraries. The first draft of the book was about 150,000 words and it was nothing like good enough to publish. When we got back to London that summer, the publisher's literary adviser broke the news to me over a drink at his flat. He began by asking me whether I had read the Bible right through from cover to cover, and whether I liked Dickens and Priestley and Evelyn Waugh. And then he enquired: 'Tell me, have you ever considered farming as a career?'

I said: 'It was absolutely shattering. For a long time I couldn't bring myself to write another sentence. Not even a letter to my family. But afterwards I went over the material again and I began to see what the literary adviser had been talking about. That autumn I came back to Skye as usual and tramped and climbed in the Cuillins and worked hard every day. After a couple more winters, I finished the book and it was accepted.

'I'll never forget the day when the post van arrived with the letter from my agents. It was January. The hills were white with snow and the washing, hanging out there on the line, was as stiff as a board. The sun was shining and I was sitting outside at a card table, eating bread and soup. When I opened the envelope and read it, I shouted "Hurray!" and danced round and round the table like a Red Indian.

'Postie was highly amused and said that he wished all his letters had the same effect on the recipients. "The wee brown envelopes with windows in them don't make people feel like dancing," said Hamish. "Except with temper, maybe."

'So you see,' said I, 'even for someone like myself, in search of the simple life, it hasn't been roses all the way. You and I have each gone out into the wilderness for forty days and nights and come back changed, hopefully wiser, men.'

Sebastian suggested that if I had nothing better to do I might like to spend the night. Cold and damp though the cottage was, the prospect of renewing its acquaintance delighted me and I accepted without a moment's hesitation.

The next morning we heard on Sebastian's radio that the overnight gales had reached eighty miles an hour. The rain during the night was terrific, showering my bedroom windows like a high-pressure fire hose. But, despite the storm, I slept soundly at last and woke at seven, refreshed and hungry for breakfast.

We drove the nine miles to Portree where Sebastian shopped for the week and posted his letters. After that we made a grand tour of the north, travelling anti-clockwise from Portree to Staffin and Duntuilm, and back by way of Uig and the west.

Outside Portree, we drew up at the site of a Celtic fort known as Dun Gerashader, and I stood with my back to the wind and made a sketch of it. Then I sketched the Old Man of Storr, a great leaning rock pinnacle, which up till then Sebastian had only seen from a distance. He was amazed to discover that the Storr Rock, which itself is 160 feet high, is set at more than 2,000 feet above sea level. But he was even more impressed by the queer rock formations we found later among the windswept gullies of the Quirang, off the Staffin road.

A white-painted sign with the warning DANGEROUS CLIFF printed in large red capitals caught our attention. But Sebastian would not be satisfied unless we explored the cliff, danger or no danger, so we climbed the high wire netting and galloped to the top, where we found a wonderful panorama of the Torridon hills and a rough blue sea which looked as if it had been dashed in with a few rapid strokes of a house painter's brush. All round us, herring gulls drifted on the wind, alighting on hairbreadth ledges far away along the sheer, brown cliff-face. The gulls made no sound as they traced invisible paths across the wind-torn blue sky.

Sebastian confessed that he found the gulls dreadfully eerie. He said: 'Did you know that Roger Whittaker has just made a record of ''Over the Sea to Skye''? He whistles the melody and does impressions of the sea-birds' cries. And now, you see, the gulls are ashamed of their own voices. Perhaps we should bring a portable gramophone up here one day and teach them to imitate Roger Whittaker!'

We passed old men and women standing at the open doors of cottages set well back off the road. Some paid no heed to us, or so it appeared. Others waved. But they all turned to follow the car's progress until it had disappeared from sight. The strange red car

would give them something to talk about. Who could be driving about Skye in December that they did not recognise? Somebody's relations perhaps? Surely not tourists, for the hotels at Staffin and Duntuilm were closed for the winter.

'I don't really feel like a tourist,' Sebastian remarked, and he added between clenched teeth, 'I don't want to be taken for one, either.' I said: 'But we aren't tourists. We are vagabonds at heart, students of nature wandering the length and breadth of this island in search of beauty and solitude and wonderful impressions.'

Sebastian sniggered and pretended to be sick. 'Ugh! I hope that's meant to be funny! You make us sound like a couple of pains in the neck.'

The pea-green-and-yellow turf, patched with islands of brown withered bracken, was dotted about with tiny white crofts, each with a black roof, like splashes of guano, shining in the strong sunlight. The sea foamed and glittered and huge masses of cloud piled up behind the mainland hills. Others streamed by in ragged sheets, brilliantly lit where the sunlight struck them as they passed overhead. A mile or so further on, we stopped for elevenses at the base of the Quirang, only to discover that Sebastian had left the coffee flask behind on the kitchen table.

It didn't matter, except to Sebastian who damned his carelessness. 'God,' he exclaimed, 'here you are, driving me all over Skye and I can't even remember to bring the sodding thermos!'

Instead, we set off to explore the Quirang. Sebastian sprinted ahead up the steep grassy hill in gigantic space-devouring strides like a stag, while I hobbled away in the opposite direction, not caring to compete with him. Besides, I told myself, I had been all over the place many times before.

'Meet you back here in a couple of hours,' Sebastian called out, brandishing above his head the alarm clock which he carried in his coat pocket instead of a watch. Some distance away I found a cemetery like a sheepfold, enclosed by a low dry-stone dyke. The cemetery was full of long-deserted graves, some of them marked by illegible, weathered headstones, others mere heaps of turf. It was overgrown with rank grass and thistles and seemed to me the bleakest, dreariest resting-place I had ever seen. The gravestones were pitched at all angles, like sailing boats in a stormy green sea.

My companion came back sooner than I expected, red-faced, perspiring, full of the wonders of the Quirang. He had gone right to the summit, fighting every step of the way against the wind. He told me that the wind, thundering among the Quirang's rocky crevasses and awesome monoliths, sounded like a Troll king bellowing deep down inside the mountain. He was exhilarated and talkative and assured me that the views surpassed even those from the DANGEROUS CLIFF which, we agreed, was saying something.

Sebastian munched a piece of bread and cheese while I finished a crayon sketch of Staffin Island and the low cerulean-blue hills of Shieldaig.

By the time we reached the ruins of Duntuilm Castle, the gale had worked up to a terrific force, so much so that it was virtually impossible to avoid being blown off one's feet. 'Too bad we can't photograph this wind,' said Sebastian. 'Even a picture of the sea-spray crashing up against those rocks hardly shows how hard it's blowing.' And he pulled down the eye-slit of his blue balaclava like a medieval knight preparing for a joust. 'People need to experience a wind like this to believe it,' I said. 'No matter how we strive to describe the gale, however vividly we manage it, nobody but ourselves will ever know what it was really like. Not even Roger Whittaker could do it.'

When we got to Uig harbour, Sebastian suggested that we might stop for a glass of beer. His treat. He still felt embarrassed about forgetting the coffee flask, but being something of a perfectionist, that was in his nature. So we found a pub overlooking Uig Bay and sat on padded Rexine-covered stools and drank our warm beer and watched the second half of a football match on the colour television mounted on the wall opposite the bar. Apart from the barman, a surly pot-bellied individual who served us without a word, the only other occupants were a pale unshaven boy of about eighteen and a grey-haired crofter with veined purple cheeks. The boy and the old man both wore heavy 'tackitty boots' and faded, navy dungarees creased like a concertina. They sat with their backs against the counter. While we were there, the boy consumed two pints of lager and the old man downed two more of McEwan's Export and two small whisky 'chasers'. Once or twice they exchanged a few words of Gaelic from which we gathered that we, and not the football match, were the subject of conversation.

As soon as the match ended, the pair got up and left, and from the window we saw them climb up onto a tractor parked outside the door. The boy took the wheel, the old man perching unsteadily behind him.

'It must be a dull sort of existence for someone of his age,' Sebastian remarked. 'And yet, just think of the compensations. If I weren't in this stupid muddle, between the devil and the deep-blue sea, I'd seriously consider coming here to live. I'd be a writer perhaps, or an ornithologist, or perhaps both. After all, why not?'

Sebastian had had a first-class education. He had been brought up in a cultivated atmosphere of books and good conversation. He was quick-witted and intelligent and insatiably curious. He confessed repeatedly to being lazy – a kind of intellectual spiv. He had never had to struggle, as I certainly struggled, to pass examinations at school and university. I felt that Sebastian did not understand the crofting lad's predicament, simply because he hadn't bothered to think it through. He was still too preoccupied with his own problems, mainly the spiritual conflict which the gale had temporarily blown out of him and which now returned in the stuffy, beer-soaked atmosphere of the pub.

As we drove away, I said: 'You and I are free spirits and may come and go as we please. For us, the world is an open door. We come here and enjoy the marvels of this beautiful Hebridean island without having to work for them. Now, think instead for a minute about that boy's life. He is up before dawn, working hard all day with the sheep and cattle. Dinner is at twelve. Tea at five. In the

evenings he'll come down here to the pub or else he'll stay at home
and watch television. He probably reads *The Press and Journal*'s
sports page and James Bond and Alastair Maclean. He dreams of fast
cars and glamorous women and Caribbean beaches. But whereas we
can choose to live here for a while and go away when we've had
enough, that boy stays or goes because he has to. To him, we are
just strangers from the mainland.'

The phrase appealed to Sebastian. 'Strangers from the mainland,'
he echoed. 'I like that very much. If I decide to chuck the
priesthood, I'll write a huge novel about the Hebrides and call it
that.'

That morning, before we set off round the island, Sebastian invited me to spend another night at the cottage. He did not have a car or even a bicycle, and said he was grateful for the opportunity to see places which otherwise would have been inaccessible without a tent and camping gear, none of which he had brought with him.

In the evening, we sat at the fire after dinner and talked and listened to the rain. Our conversation was rambling and disordered compared to the previous night, and suited the rambling disorder of the day. Sebastian said that he'd talked quite enough about himself and his problems by then, and he pressed me to tell a little more about my own life. He proved to be a good listener and asked questions on a great variety of subjects which gradually drew me out. 'Of all the people you've read,' he asked suddenly, apropos of nothing, 'whose work do you admire the most?'

I said that I was greatly drawn to Stephen Graham, who had been a literary tramp of the old-fashioned sort, a fluent, charming writer who wrote a lovely book about the Christian faith in pre-Bolshevik Russia called *The Way of Martha and the Way of Mary*. And I said that I had been drawn to Graham's friend and tramping-companion of later years, Vachel Lindsay. Lindsay had wandered the American Middle West exchanging his poems printed on broadsheets for food and shelter. He had felled timber and harvested wheat in Kansas and had died in 1931, disenchanted, lonely, feeling that his talents had burned out and resenting the mass popularity his verses had achieved. Stephen Graham, on the other hand, suffered no such personal doubts and lived to a ripe old age. He ended his days in London in his Soho flat, bedridden, impoverished, but rich in memories and experiences.

'I think the wanderers mean most to me,' I said. 'There's really something very attractive about such men and women. Stevenson was tremendously good when he wrote about the Cévennes and the South Seas. His novelette, *The Pavilion on the Links*, has always been a great favourite of mine, not so much because of the story, but because the hero, Frank Cassilis, was a wanderer too. Stevenson tells how Cassilis tramped all over Scotland carrying his worldly possessions in a tilt-cart pulled by a horse, and how it had been

Cassilis's "whole business to find desolate corners" far removed from the madding crowd. When I read that book, I was with Frank Cassilis all the way, sleeping among the sand dunes along the east coast, or tenting in the woods where there were wild roses, and bluebells and buttercups among the grass in springtime. I was told when I was small that buttercups and daisies were Tom Tiddler's treasure, and from the age of six or seven they were all the treasure I ever wanted in life. I wonder what our friend, the crofter's son, would make of that? He'd probably think I was an awful drip!

'I could never get along with W.H. Davies for some reason, any more than I could with Gipsy Borrow. Don't ask me why, I can't tell you. And yet, in ways, I admire Davies and George Borrow immensely. Both were committed root and branch to the tramping way. They were self-possessed, intelligent men; first-class writers with what our parents and grandparents called "good minds". How much poorer literature would be without *The Autobiography of a Super-Tramp* and *Lavengro* and *The Bible in Spain*! I am not normally envious, but how I envy Borrow's remarkable gift for languages! And Davies, going about in America with his friend, Brum, who made an art of living off the country. Vachel Lindsay's tramping philosophy, on the other hand, was more akin to Borrow than Davies. Here are Lindsay's rules of the road:

> Keep away from the Cities.
> Keep away from the railroads.
> Have nothing to do with money and carry no baggage ...
> Travel alone.
> Be neat, deliberate, chaste and civil.
> Preach the Gospel of Beauty.

'You know,' said Sebastian, 'at first meeting, you don't strike one as the vagabond type. Perhaps you're too clean and tidy. And you're clean-shaven, which doesn't seem right at all! We'll put you down for a gentleman tramp, I think. How does that suit you?'

'Well,' I said, 'we are what we are, I suppose, for all our crazy notions and philosophies. Graham used to say that Lindsay, in his broad-brimmed black hat and red neckerchief, reminded him of a tramping-violinist – whatever that may mean. I've loved the tramping life since I was a child you see, thanks to my grandmother and the strange assortment of ragamuffins who used to visit her every year.'

The idea intrigued Sebastian. And there and then he insisted that I tell him how it had all come about.

Until I was nine I lived with my parents at my grandparents' house on the River Clyde. There I met a great many of the tramps and packmen who wandered up and down the Clyde coast every summer between Glasgow and Ardrossan. My grandmother used to provide the regulars with a hot midday meal of ham and eggs and fried soda scones, which they ate out of doors. One day I remember Granny calling my mother to the window, exclaiming: 'Now just look at that man, how he sits down to his dinner like a gentleman, with his cap folded on his knee!'

The tramps told me stories and sang and made me laugh. I envied them tremendously. They had neither school nor work to go to and, moreover, judging by the tawny colour of their hands and faces, they had been spared the distasteful ritual of washing! The tramps had scarcely any possessions and they seemed to get by very satisfactorily without money. All this intrigued me enormously.

My pocket-money in those days was half a crown a week, two shillings of which my parents invested in a small Post Office deposit account. Sixpence, divided on sweets and comics, went a long way in the village shop, even in 1947. And, for the remainder, it meant nothing more to me than ever-lengthening columns of 'twos' which the postmistress wrote down in my passbook in various shades of blue ink. After a while I was told that the account contained seventeen pounds; but when I asked whether this would be enough for me to live on for the rest of my life, I was told that most certainly it would not, but that if I looked after the pennies the pounds would take care of themselves.

Being rather slow on the uptake, I was still none the wiser. 'When the book has twenty pounds in it,' I persisted, 'will that last me for ever?' Nobody appeared very sure how much one did need to live for ever, but everyone shook their heads and smiled knowingly and left me feeling even more mystified than before.

There and then, however, I decided that the Post Office books belonging to the tramps must be altogether different things from mine.

Above all, I was impressed by the tramps' obviously carefree attitude to life. My father and my mother's elder brothers had all gone off to fight in the War. Until that moment their lives had been placid, routine and fairly uneventful. What they saw and experienced had had a terrible effect on them. Their outlook became sombre and uncertain. They spoke gravely, with trepidation, about subjects like The Future, which I couldn't begin to comprehend. By contrast, the tramping fraternity were like the birds in the trees. They dwelt entirely in the present, and lived naturally and uncaringly from day to day.

I can picture some of the tramps here and now, seated a little way from the house on a square patch of lawn flanked by rhododendrons and a high beech hedge, and herbaceous borders filled with orange and red and purple lupins. On the far side of the lupins there was a green-painted summer seat with decorative wrought-iron armrests and feet, and here the tramps ate their lunch while I stood by listening to their conversation and the fat, brown bumble-bees droned sleepily back and forth among the flowers.

One morning there was a strong southerly wind which sent the clouds flying across the sky like a scene photographed with a time-lapse camera. Two packmen had stopped at the house on their way to Port Glasgow or Greenock, and were drinking tea from smoke-blackened tin mugs. I asked the older man, 'Where will you go this summer?' He grinned and got up and flung his old ragged bonnet high into the air so that the wind caught it and blew it far away across the garden. 'That's where we're going,' he said.

The incident made a deep and lasting impression. Ever since, I have disliked walking with a fixed destination in mind; just as I prefer not to consult maps or gazetteers telling me the history of churches or old buildings or the various other landmarks I might find along the way. W.H. Hudson, whose works I discovered in my early twenties, at the beginning of his charming book *Afoot in England* advised those who travel for pleasure 'not to look at a

guidebook until the place it treats of has been explored and left behind'. Hudson went on: 'In recalling those scenes which have given me the greatest happiness, the images of which are most vivid and lasting, I find that most of them are scenes or objects which were discovered, as it were, by chance, which I had not heard of, or else had heard of and forgotten, or which I had not expected to see'.

My happiest journeys, like Hudson's, have been those undertaken spontaneously without too much care or forethought. And I have found the best travel books to be those full of unexpected adventures woven into a fabric of haphazard wanderings which take on a life of their own, so that the reader, like the traveller, is carried along by an irresistible momentum, like the tramp's old bonnet I saw whipped away by the south wind.

Starting with Hudson, I gathered a small collection of tramping literature written for the most part by men and women whose feelings about the great outdoors reflected strong feelings and ideas of my own. Edward Verrall Lucas's evergreen anthology, *The Open Road*, became a lifelong favourite. I read Stevenson's travels in the Cévennes and Belloc's account of a 750-mile pilgrimage on foot across France and Italy, *The Path to Rome*. Nicholas Vachel Lindsay, the American poet and artist, fascinated me, and I fell under the spell of his idealistic *Adventures While Preaching the Gospel of Beauty* and the more practical *A Handy Guide for Beggars*. When I was twenty-six, as the result of a chance meeting with an old blind horse-trader from Vladicavcaz called Agube Gudsow, I found Stephen Graham's first book, *A Vagabond in the Caucasus*.

It surprised me to discover that this prolific, now sadly neglected writer never wrote a book of travels about Scotland where he was born in 1884. In spite of his Edinburgh background and his youthful, rather sickly passion for Thomas Carlyle, the wider horizons of Russia, the Balkans and North America drew Graham away from his homeland from the beginning. He tramped 400 miles round the Black Sea shores and followed General Sherman's route down through Georgia. With his friend of later years, the Springfield poet Vachel Lindsay, he crossed the Glacier National Park from Montana into Canada in 1921, and wrote about their journey in a marvellous book called *Tramping with a Poet in the Rockies*, which Freya Stark gave me for Christmas a few years ago in Asolo.

Stephen Graham's approach to his wanderings, I found, corresponded almost exactly to my own. He never set out to chalk up the miles purely for the sake of walking. In his own words, 'I for my part hardly believe in tramping for tramping's sake, but in living with Nature for what that is worth. To sleep under the stars, to live with the river that sings as it flows ...' Lindsay, like Graham, covered some tremendous distances in his day, trudging across Kansas and the Middle West. He would leave home almost as if to post a letter, and finish up by walking 1,000 miles. This is very much the way of a labourer I met not long ago in Perthshire, whose ambition was to set off with his backpack and his dog and just keep on going.

Like Stephen Graham, I enjoy being out and away for no other reason; being able to throw down my pack and stretch out in the sun and doze or daydream or sketch the scenery as I please. It does not matter very much if I end the day having tramped ten miles or thirty. Being out of doors among the hills is the great thing.

A few months before his death, Agube Gudsow, then just short of ninety, gave me as a present his unpublished manuscript entitled *The Unknown Land*. The work was a mixture of Caucasian folklore, tribal history and fragments of autobiography describing his childhood on the Terek River. Agube had been brought up in a remote village and could remember days when a chieftain's wealth was measured by horses, sheep and cartridges. Agube's tales fired my imagination and imbued me with a desire to travel among the mountains. The great Scottish hills lay at our doorstep – or, at any rate, within easy reach – and after reading Gudsow and Graham I saw them through changed eyes. But it was not until I began to live for months at a time on Skye and other parts of the Highlands that I began to appreciate the magic and romance of our own hills.

For years I had taken them for granted. I had scarcely bothered to look at them, let alone think of exploring them for myself. Slowly but surely, I became aware of an entire new world. Tramping in the Highlands grew to be an obsession, and I covered hundreds of miles on foot in all weathers, at every season of the year. The moors, which had once seemed bleak and lifeless, now revealed themselves as a veritable wonderland, a glorious wild garden where in summer countless varieties of tiny wildflowers grew, besides the lichens, mosses, shrubs and heather. Their delicate subtle colours delighted me as much as the extraordinary variety of shapes and textures and the continuously changing light.

The wildlife of the Highlands, especially the Red deer, interested me more and more, and I spent months sketching them in the open, or else simply lying out in the heather watching them through a telescope or binoculars. Although I realised that I could never be content to devote my life to perfecting the technique of stalking pictures as an end in itself, there was an incomparable delight in the days I spent observing deer. Those days live on in the memory and imagination and they appear, now as then, as oases of perfect tranquillity and pleasure.

Most of my walking has from the outset been done alone, for to be honest I find that companions, however well I know them, are a distraction. Even so, I have often thought, sitting high up on a hillside in Skye or Perthshire, what fun it would be to have someone to turn to and share the pleasure of the view.

When I was five I had a small blue bicycle which I used to ride along the entire length of the woods behind our house on a winding path of green turf. In summer my mother and my aunt sometimes walked there in the evening. Aunt Emily was very fond of honeysuckle, and I remember how she used to pull down the flowers to her brow and breathe the heavy fragrance with her eyes half-closed.

The road that ran past the garden was hardly used by motor traffic in those days, and in summer the grass sprouted in tiny clumps from cracks in its metalled surface made by the heavily tracked Army vehicles going to and from the nearby gunsite. I remember lying flat on my stomach on the warm tarmacadam with the road at eye-level, seeing it vanish to infinity through the dancing waves of heat reflections. Or again, stretching out in a cornfield at the back of the house, staring up into the depths of dark-blue sky at a tiny aeroplane which droned like a bee among the gently floating white and copper clouds.

The sickly-sweet scented honeysuckle, the heatwaves shimmering on the road and the trembling whine of the plane high above the fields have remained for me symbols of youth, innocence and freedom.

There is no doubt that the wanderlust in me was kindled by stories which my parents, aunts and uncles encouraged me to read, or else read to me, as a small boy. Aunt Emily, my mother's elder sister, was one of the kindest, gentlest people I have ever known. She spent hours reading aloud to me marvellously thrilling adventures, such as *The Gorilla Hunters, The Coral Island* and *The Count of Monte Cristo*. Aunt Emily read so well and brought these tales so vividly to life that I used to identify with the characters to an extent which alternately amused and horrified my parents. When the Count was thrown into the dungeons, for instance, I wanted nothing to eat for days but bread and water. And when Ballantyne's hardy trio of adventurers arrived in the heart of the gorilla country, I craved for blood-red meat and took to wearing my long-tailed grey school shirt outside my trousers with an enormous machete made from a rusty scythe-blade under my leather belt.

These crazes were short-lived, but the desire for wandering never waned. From the gorilla-hunter, Ralph Rover, I learned a profound distaste for any form of gainful employment. Looking back, I can well imagine how my poor parents must have loathed Ballantyne and his beguiling descriptions of Ralph Rover's comfortable Victorian apartments where he lived between his expeditions on a private income of three hundred pounds a year. Ralph was portrayed at twenty-two as a studious, unworldly youth, who spent his time roaming the countryside and contributing articles on natural history to the journals of provincial learned societies. His life was the model of what I hoped mine might one day become. As a recipe for a wanderer's happy existence, Ralph's self-indulgent lifestyle represented for me the acme of perfection.

Something of Ralph Rover remains a part of me to this day, and I still turn every so often to my old tattered copy of *The Gorilla Hunters* with nostalgia and feelings of real affection. But I know now what I had then completely failed to realise, that without my upbringing at Erskine Cottage and its background of sturdy integrity and understanding, the opportunity in later years to travel and paint and write might never have existed.

The countryside surrounding the house has changed irrevocably. A road has cut the woods in half and a motorway linking Glasgow and the Firth of Clyde runs within a few hundred yards of the front gate. The fields which once separated us from the village are a maze of side roads and new houses. To a large extent the old feeling of privacy has gone, and yet the house itself and the garden are the same as they were when I was a boy, except, of course, they now appear much smaller. My roots are there, however, and they always will be.

My grandparents bought the house in 1923 and it has belonged to our family ever since. Grandpa, who had been a great expert in cultivating tomatoes and chrysanthemums, laid out the garden. All through the years I knew him, he suffered from pernicious anaemia and, as old people in the village used to say, 'wandered in his mind'. He passed his days sitting quietly in his armchair staring into space or walking slowly round the garden. What his thoughts were, nobody knew.

Once I found him kneeling beside some drills of newly planted seed potatoes. He was turning the dry earth over and over in his hands and there was a strange, rapturous expression on his face. When he saw me, he smiled and held up a little heap of earth cupped in his hands. He put his face to the earth and inhaled deeply, just as Aunt Emily used to inhale the heavy-scented honeysuckle. Then Grandpa held out his hands to me. 'Smell it,' he said. 'Smell the good ground. It's beautiful ... so beautiful.'

Whatever feelings I have for the moors and hills owe a great deal to experiences like these. As a child I learned an awareness for the value of life, and the fact that there is beauty in every living thing, however humble. Even so, I can't pretend that I have always treated nature with respect; but at least I've always known that I should. In this sense, I suppose, a man can be every bit as much an explorer when he gazes into the heart of a wildflower as he is when crossing the immeasurable wastes of ice or sand....

Our cottage, despite its changed surroundings, is still that most ideal place: one which I may close the door upon and leave, and return to, as and when I please, with equal feelings of happiness and anticipation.

My journeys about Scotland – in Skye, the Perthshire hills, Inverness, Ross-shire, Argyllshire and north Kintyre – almost all of them began from there.

The spring and summer tramps I made all over the Highlands have been some of the best things in my life. It's always wonderful to be setting off somewhere again.... Going on foot, with a knapsack and sketchbooks and enough food for two or three days. Driving round in a motor-car simply isn't the same as walking. You cover more ground, but you don't *feel* it. Impressions come and go too quickly to mean much. A car comes between you and Mother Earth. I need to feel the ground under my feet. Mark my words, when you've tramped thirty or forty miles in the wind and rain, and dreamed dreams lying out absolutely exhausted in the heather, you'll want nothing more to do with cars. It sounds pretty arch, and even masochistic, but it's true, all the same....

I remember once walking up through Glen Sligachan with some friends who had come up the day before from London. It was a glorious spring morning and the scenery, as you can imagine, was magnificent. After a long walk, we got to a place where there was a big snowfield and a waterfall gushing down nearby. The couple I was with had done hardly any walking in their lives. They were totally exhausted. Whipped and done for, as the Americans would say.

We undressed and showered under the waterfall and then we rubbed ourselves down with handfuls of snow. It felt marvellous. You simply cannot believe how good it felt! The whole thing went straight to their heads like champagne and I can still see them, racing about like over-excited children, pelting one another with snowballs.

Going about Skye in Sebastian's company had been a pleasant interlude. It was fun pointing out things and places which evoked happy memories, and just as much fun seeing the delight he took in them. To Sebastian it was all thrillingly different. But our brief journey, much as I enjoyed it, was in some ways a depressing experience, for whenever I glimpsed a familiar landmark, I thought immediately about the people connected with it, many of whom were long-since dead and gone.

Skye, even when I lived there in the 1960s, had boasted more than its fair share of characters, and now that they were gone the island was a poorer place in consequence. All this happened, let me add, in less than a decade.

Over and over I have heard it repeated, 'We will never see their like again'. I am afraid it is true. Outstanding personalities such as Dame Flora MacLeod, Danny the Seannachie, the naturalist, Seton Gordon and Colonel Jock MacDonald were the products of a vanished era, who had spent much of their early lives in a world largely devoid of mass communication.

Dame Flora told me how in the 1870s, when she was a child, travelling from London to Skye by land and sea still involved a long and fairly arduous expedition. Fifty years on, instead of picking up the telephone, people still kept in touch mainly by writing letters to one another. Seton Gordon recalled a time on Skye when the *fourth* daily delivery of post arrived at Upper Duntuilm after 10 p.m.

In the evenings, when the day's work was finished, the crofting families gathered round the fire and talked instead of staring fixedly in drab silence at a television screen. It seems to me particularly strange that the modern television audience in the Hebrides actually prefers to watch celebrities talking to a chat-show host rather than make conversation as they once did amongst themselves. The universal craving for information about the world at large has gradually eroded people's concern for family life and the affairs of the local community. It would be ridiculous to suggest that family or community activities might be neglected entirely; but I think few would disagree that the emphasis of concern has changed, arguably for the worse. Social life has become a reach-me-down, second-hand affair. Observation is taking the place of participation.

A world of increasing uniformity is hardly likely to produce the colourful, 'offbeat' personalities of days gone by. We live in the age of the common denominator – some would say, the *lowest* common denominator. If our present and future generations throw up characters in the traditional sense of the word, they will be of a totally different breed.

I have been told that this outlook is excessively and unjustifiably gloomy. My friends say, 'Your ideal is the romantic ideal. You can't pull the handbrake on progress. Twenty years, two hundred years, what's the difference? *Tout c'est changé*. Time passes and romantic dreamers like you become further and further separated from reality. You are one of those unhappy creatures who enshrine a glorified vision of the past, feel out of step with the present and dread the future.'

Like it or not, I am forced to admit that much of what they say is true. Change, not to be confused with so-called progress, is inevitable and in many respects is for the better.

Take the Skye crofters in the nineteenth century as an example. Their life was one of desperate hardship, a degree of hardship inconceivable to modern generations. Families often shared the same damp, unventilated hovel with cattle, pigs and other livestock. But compared to the poor of the towns and cities, such as Dundee or Edinburgh or Glasgow, the crofter's family as a rule had had more to eat. And if their diet of herring, oatmeal and potatoes was repetitive, it was also fairly nourishing.

The crofting families made their own entertainment and in turn they entertained each other. The *ceiladh* kept alive oral traditions. Almost every community had its *seannachie*, the bardic chronicler who recited stirring tales of past deeds and great events, 'stories of witchcraft, stories of haunted places'.

I can recall as clearly as though it were yesterday my first meeting with Danny McLachlan, the *seannachie* from Loch Snizort. One cloudless spring morning, Danny and I sat on a grassy knoll looking out over the pale blue water, and I listened, fascinated, as the old man talked. His voice was gentle and melodious. As he spoke, he beat time with the words, striking the turf with his long *cromach*. His diction was precise and clear. He spoke slowly and deliberately, giving a prolonged dramatic emphasis to certain key words or phrases. It was an experience I shall never forget.

Danny was by then well into his seventies. He was a tall man with gaunt features, deep-set pale-blue eyes and a grizzled lantern jaw. For some years he had suffered from a cataract in both eyes, but his hearing was well-nigh perfect and he was fit and remarkably agile for a man of his age. The local doctor who introduced us told me that although he appeared to exist on a diet of porridge and fresh air, Danny had the constitution of an ox. With his old leather helmet pulled down low over his brow, and its fur-lined ear-flaps

turned up like horns on either side, he was like the reincarnation of a Viking warrior.

The Skye legends and stories which Danny told me were mixed at random with other curious recollections of his own. During the First World War, he had served aboard Admiral Beatty's flagship at the Battle of Jutland, and it was Danny's proud boast that he could still recite Beatty's famous Jutland address in its entirety. He had met several members of the Tsar's family at the same period and he still received occasional letters from the Grand Duchess Xenia who lived at a grace-and-favour apartment in Hampton Court Palace.

Seton Gordon, who was also a friend of the Duchess, told me how he had visited Danny's croft one day and found the old man deeply distressed, anguishing over his reply to a letter which had arrived from Xenia that morning. Nothing Danny had written would satisfy him, and in the end Seton Gordon advised him to put aside his pen and paper and go for a long walk over the hill to clear his brain. When Danny returned an hour or so later, he sat down and finished his letter without any further difficulty.

Not long afterwards, Danny told Seton Gordon: 'You were right enough. When I began to write after the walk in the fresh air, it was like a river flowing!'

Seton Gordon was a tremendously interesting man in his own right. During my first winter on Skye, I had the good fortune to be introduced to him, and I visited him from time to time at his house on the windswept north coast near Duntuilm.

We did not meet very frequently, but we wrote to each other a good deal about subjects of mutual interest: the birdlife around Sligachan, for example, and believe it or not, the weather. As a naturalist, the weather was of great importance to Seton, and our discussions ranged far beyond the usual perfunctory remarks all of us have scribbled at one time or another on the back of a holiday postcard. Sometimes his letters enclosed sunshine charts. These were semi-circular sheets of paper on which the number of hours and the intensity of daily sunshine were visually recorded by means of a burning-glass.

Seton also took a great interest in the monthly rainfall, which I measured from a long, funnel-shaped copper gauge buried in the peaty ground in front of the cottage. The wettest month I can remember was March 1968, when it rained almost continuously day and night for thirty-one days. In the damp, draughty cottage we felt as though we were marooned in Noah's Ark. The wooden bridge over the burn was flooded for a week, and Hamish the postman used to get out of his small red van and roll up his sleeves to test the depth of water with his bare arm before he judged it safe to cross! That year, I believe, the total rainfall on Skye exceeded 140 inches.

Often when I visited Duntuilm, Seton told me fascinating stories about his days spent observing the golden eagle, the noble species with which his name will always be associated. Both in conversation and in his books, he tended to be secretive about the eagles' nesting places, and I think rightly so. Seton was an excellent photographer, and the black and white studies he made of eagles and sea-birds testified to his unrivalled knowledge of their habitat and his practical skill and daring. Some of these detailed close-ups were achieved at considerable personal risk. Both he and his first wife, the late Audrey Pease, devoted an enormous amount of time and patience to their work. In a remote deer forest in Sutherland, the Gordons spent 500 hours observing a pair of eagles over a period of five years.

Seton's book, *The Golden Eagle*, describes the hardships of a field-naturalist's life: 'Many hours of watching during frost and snow, bitter winter gales and storms of stinging hail ... offset by hours of brilliant sunshine and warmth'. Of a prolonged eagle-watch, he wrote: 'I have expended much energy in reaching my observation post, and during the eight years I calculate I have walked upwards of 1,500 miles, during almost all of them accompanied by my collie, Dugie ...'

There were many memorable days, such as one 'glowing and wondrous' morning in June when Seton left home at 4 a.m. and climbed to an eyrie occupied by a single eaglet. He wrote: 'Now, as I looked at the downy eaglet, shining white as a snowball below me, the sun each moment gained strength, and the heated air was scented with alpine plants – the high hills were fragrant and radiant'.

Brief examples like these hardly begin to tell the range and brilliance of Seton's writing, which was based on the careful records he had kept over half a century and more: the daily weather, where he had been and what he had seen and done, what flowers and shrubs were in bloom and what birds and animals were about. He was a perceptive, indefatigable observer of wild nature, and an inveterate note-taker. It amused me that his Christian name, spelled backwards, reads 'Notes', and to my mind this trivial observation highlighted the indispensable ingredient of his *modus operandi*.

My knowledge of birds being fairly limited, I seldom felt confident enough to question, far less dispute, Seton's authoritative views, except once when we had a minor difference of opinion about an adventure which occurred at Sligachan in the early spring of 1970.

What happened was this. A lovely mild morning dawned, with an almost cloudless blue sky. After breakfast I went down to the burn – still in my carpet slippers – and sat on a stone and watched the bright water tumbling and flashing in the sunlight. Everything was still and peaceful. I clearly remember thinking, 'How wonderful it all is, how gloriously content! I must never forget this spring morning, for this is surely one of the happiest, most wonderful moments of my whole life.'

As I sat there, I noticed out of the corner of my eye two tiny specks in the sky directly above the cottage. The birds flew at great speed. At first I imagined they were house-martins, but they were so far away and their movements were so rapid that I couldn't be sure. Suddenly one of the birds dived down and vanished behind the cottage. Its companion circled above me for a while longer and then flew away. A moment or two later, my wife appeared at the cottage door. 'Come quickly,' she shouted. 'There's a bird in the kitchen.' Just as I got inside, I heard a frantic scuffling behind the tins lining the top of the kitchen dresser. The bird flashed across the room, striking the window pane with a loud thump and dropped down under the table. It was stunned but, as far as we could tell, uninjured. To my surprise, I saw it was a swift.

While I held the swift gently cupped in my hands, my wife fetched one of our bird books from the sitting-room. The coloured illustration and a brief description confirmed the swift's identity. I carried it outside and waited for it to regain consciousness. As the swift came round, it gripped my fingers where they join the palm and clung there for about a minute, blinking and slowly opening and closing its beak. Holding the hand to which it clung upright, I slowly took my other hand away and let it go.

The circumstances and the thrill of holding the live bird, feeling its tiny rapid heart-beat, meant far more to me than the fact that it was a swift, for at the time I had no idea how unusual our experience had been. When I telephoned Seton some days later and described the event, he sounded extremely doubtful. He explained that the earliest time of year that the swift had been sighted in Scotland was mid-April, and that that sighting had taken place eighty years ago. The sighting I claimed pre-dated that one by three weeks. Seton questioned me again and again about the bird's size, its colour-markings and the shape and length of its wings. 'Did you put it down on the ground before it flew off?' he asked. I repeated what had happened, but Seton remained sceptical and said he felt sure the bird must have been a house-martin.

A good clear photograph would have settled the matter, but, as luck would have it, my wife had exposed the last of the spool the day before and we had no more film left. I had nothing to measure the bird's length with except my handspan which, when fully extended, is exactly nine inches. The swift was about one and a half inches shorter, perhaps a fraction more. Its wingspan, we reckoned, was about the same as its body length. I wrote an article for *The Field* immediately afterwards while the facts were still fresh in my mind; but it went unnoticed, so I assume that the ornithologists who read it must have agreed with Seton that I had made a mistake. I don't entirely blame them, for, reading over these paragraphs, they sound a bit like the fisherman's story about the one that got away.

Seton's house in Skye stood some way back from the coast road down which Sebastian and I had driven in the gale. It was comfortable and spacious, with books and pictures everywhere. I do not remember the garden very well, for most of our conversations took place indoors.

One winter's afternoon at Duntuilm, we sat in the dining-room with its sea view and talked for hours over the delicious tea of freshly baked oven-scones and home-made strawberry jam which Betty Gordon had provided. We talked until well after sunset and our faces were barely visible in the gloaming. That day Seton was dressed colourfully in his faded kilt and grey-blue Prince of Wales check kilt-jacket and waistcoat. He wore a scarlet flannel shirt and a Gamboge-yellow tie and heavy black brogues with fringed leather flaps covering the laces. He was in excellent spirits and scarcely drew breath, telling stories one after another in his high-pitched, slightly tremulous voice. When he laughed he bared his teeth and gums, very much like the late Lord Stockton, and his grey moustache further heightened this resemblance.

Seton's stories were astonishing for their wealth of carefully observed and recollected detail. He surveyed his friends and acquaintances, and indeed the whole of life, with a naturalist's acute eye. Whether he was describing the way of ravens or eagles, or reminiscing about his days at university, it hardly mattered. The approach was very much the same.

At Eton, he met and befriended Denys Finch-Hatton, a younger son of the Earl of Winchelsea, who subsequently lived in Kenya as a professional hunter and achieved a wider posthumous fame as the lover and confidante of the Danish authoress, Karen Blixen. The friendship between Seton and Denys continued at Oxford. They were both keen golfers; Finch-Hatton captained the Oxford team of which Seton was a member. That afternoon at Duntuilm, Seton told me an amusing anecdote about an Oxford–Cambridge golf match which illustrated Finch-Hatton's sportsmanship and his gift for quick-witted repartee. He had conceded a longish putt, giving his opponent the chance to fight back at a critical stage of the game. One of the spectators, an Oxford supporter, stepped forward and angrily reprimanded Finch-Hatton. 'My dear fellow, do try to remember that you are playing for your side and not the other.' To which Finch-Hatton replied coolly, 'And you, my dear sir, kindly remember that you are playing for neither.'

Another of Seton's close friends at Oxford was Prince Felix Yousopoff, a cousin of the Tsar, who later helped to murder Rasputin. One of Seton's most terrifying experiences was being driven at high speed by Yousopoff round a succession of narrow mountain roads in the Caucasus, some of which bordered sheer precipices many hundreds of feet high. As they hurtled along, the tyres screaming at every hairpin bend, Seton noticed vultures circling slowly overhead, as he observed wryly, 'without doubt in anticipation of a meal'. During their long journey across Russia in 1911 they passed through no fewer than thirty-two vast estates owned by Yousopoff's family. In Moscow, the winter snow had begun to melt and the streets lay ankle-deep in mud and slush. Seton's strongest impressions were of leaden skies, the endlessly tolling bells and the peasants trudging by. 'Everyone moved very slowly,' he told me. 'They reminded me very much of people here in the Hebrides, going slowly with their heads bowed and leaning forward into the wind.'

In his book, *The Charm of Skye* published in 1929, he referred again and again to 'leaden' skies, the driving rain and the 'furiously whirling' snow – wintry images which recalled his Russian travels and the Spitzbergen archipelago which he visited in 1921 as photographer to an Oxford University expedition.

When I asked Seton whether he had ever discussed Rasputin's murder with Yousopoff, he said that he had once, but only very briefly. One evening in London Yousopoff began to tell the story, which Seton was anxious to hear at first hand; but halfway through, the doorbell rang and an unexpected visitor arrived. As a result, much to Seton's regret, this unique version of the story was never finished.

One of Seton's closest friends on Skye was the late Colonel Jock MacDonald. Like Seton, Jock was steeped in Hebridean folklore. Both men were accomplished pipers and judged most of the Skye piping competitions, besides other important contests throughout the Highlands. 'Colonel Jock', as he was known to everybody, had a heart of gold and a marvellously original sense of humour. He was probably the last of the great Skye characters and became a legend in his own lifetime. Jock was short and sturdy, ruddy-complexioned, with twinkling blue eyes and a penetrating gaze. He invariably wore a kilt, a dark blue beret and hobnailed brogues with enormous toecaps like regulation army boots. One of his favourite kilts had been made from a length of threadbare curtain material, and the concertina pleats were peppered with tiny holes and singe marks due to his habit of standing with his back to the wood fire in the drawing-room. He smoked a short-stemmed pipe and enjoyed his evening dram of whisky which on a cold winter's night he sometimes mixed with Bovril.

Jock was a great extrovert, fond of an audience and yet in other ways he seemed a very private, even shy man. Few people, I believe, except his closest friends, really knew what he was thinking. Jock's abrupt manner was apt to catch the unwary listener offguard, but no matter how gruff or outspoken he might appear, his bright beady eye and throaty chuckle neutralised many a remark which otherwise would have caused offence. I cannot remember ever having a conversation with him when he failed to transform the most humdrum situation into something memorable.

One dark stormy November night, Jock arrived at my cottage in his battered green van with a set of bagpipes under his arm, parcelled up in a thick felt dressing-gown. When he got indoors, he carefully unwrapped the pipes, donned the dressing-gown and sat down by the fire with a glass in his hand. He shivered repeatedly, making it very obvious that he was cold, and he kept turning and glaring at the sitting-room door, which was set about an inch above the bare floorboards. 'I don't care for draughts,' he remarked, shrugging with feigned discomfort, 'that is, unless they are confined to a tumbler.'

Of course, he had been having me on. We talked for a while and after that Jock reached for his pipes. One of the drones was missing and the hole in the pouch had been plugged with a sherry cork. He made a great thing of this deficiency, blowing up the bag, taking the pipes apart and laboriously reassembling them as though wrestling with an hysterical, squawking bird that was all spindly legs and beak and totally uncontrollable. But when he began to play, pacing gravely up and down the room, the vaudeville atmosphere immediately changed and I was treated to a masterly performance. The tone of these pipes was light and high-pitched, quite different to others I had heard.

Jock explained that the pipes were specially designed to be played indoors; they were chamber-pipes, a type originally developed by the famous eighteenth-century piping family, the McCrimmons, and the tunes he played that night were all McCrimmon tunes. It is true that full-powered bagpipes sound far sweeter when they are played outside in their natural Highland setting. But that evening held a great charm for me: the strain of the pipes; the wind howling about the cottage; the incessant patter of rain; the wavering yellow lamplight; and the quaint goblin figure clad in his trailing robe and Tam o' Shanter, casting weird shadows on the walls.

Most of the stories told about Colonel Jock have tended to be episodic. This is not really surprising, for he was larger than life, with something of the grease-paint, stand-up comic about him. The theatrical character with which he affronted the world at large was kept alive in latter years by Jock's own shrewd awareness of his eccentric reputation. There had been much in his life which the tinderbox sparkle and oddly dignified ebullience concealed. The funniest men are often keepers of some deep, unspoken grief, and Jock was no exception.

The great gloomy Victorian Gothic house where he lived created a perfect stage set. Eventually the crippling expense of maintaining it forced the MacDonalds to run their home in the summer months as a private hotel. To begin with Jock loathed the prospect of strangers descending upon him in busloads, usurping his privacy, interfering with his routine.

One morning he stomped into the dining-room and sat down to his breakfast of porridge and eggs beside a harmless, rather vulgar man who was noisily gobbling a plate of mushy cornflakes. Jock endured the spectacle for a few minutes, all the while fixing his

neighbour with a coldly disapproving stare. At last he leaned forward and snapped, 'Look here, if you won't eat in a civilised manner with your mouth shut, I intend to throw you out of the window!' The embarrassed guest meekly obeyed, though his feelings are best left to the imagination.

Jock's taste for practical jokes took various forms. He kept a good many animals about the place: spaniels of all ages and colours, an enormous deerhound, a goose whom Jock christened 'Jim the Tory' and Ozzie the owl, who perched on a coatstand in the drawing-room with a copy of *The Times* spread out strategically below him.

The walls of the entrance hall and staircase were lined with big-game trophies from Africa and India where Jock had served with a cavalry regiment at Poona. (It could only have been Poona!) There were stuffed birds of prey, including hawks and eagles, and sometimes Jock would perch Ozzie among them where he sat motionless and unblinking, a willing stooge in the comedy which followed. Jock would reappear shepherding a flock of elderly spinsters who had asked to be shown the collection. As he mounted the great staircase step by step, Jock would describe the various specimens, urging the ladies to have a good close look at each in turn. Then he would arrive in front of Ozzie, who would suddenly flap his wings and hiss and scare Jock's timorous following half to death.

The goose was to my certain knowledge reprieved for at least six Christmases, until in the end he was beyond eating and died of old age. An Airedale, whose name I cannot remember, also featured in several extraordinary episodes. The story goes that on one occasion, when the MacDonalds had been invited to a wedding, Mrs MacDonald discovered that her fur coat had been ravaged by moths and looked as though it were suffering from a bad attack of mange. The coat was dark musquash, but, nothing daunted, she solved the problem by shearing the dog and sticking its bright-orange clippings to the bald patches with Copydex. The effect, I was told, was startling to put it mildly.

During an election campaign, the Airedale, or one of its predecessors, could be seen trotting about Portree with a placard dangling from his collar bearing an inscription in large letters which read: I AM A CLEAN DOG, BUT YOU ARE A DIRTY DOG IF YOU DON'T VOTE

FOR LORD MALCOLM DOUGLAS-HAMILTON! There are scores of anecdotes in a similar vein, enough to fill a book, I daresay.

Although Jock was to most people on Skye a notorious eccentric and a source of endless gossip and hilarity, I always felt that other sides of his personality were far more interesting. He was well-travelled, he was a fluent Gaelic speaker, a devout Christian and an excellent piper. Moreover, he was a fine naturalist, a fact to which Seton Gordon testified, and he was a mine of information about the old Skye life and its traditions.

Mrs MacDonald was every bit as entertaining as her husband and consequently was much in demand as a public speaker. In November 1967 I was invited to give a talk to the Portree branch of the Women's Rural Institute. Mrs MacDonald, needless to say, was in the chair. My talk was about the explorer, Speke, and his devoted Scots companion James Augustus Grant. The audience listened attentively, although judging by the brief, disjointed clatter of applause which followed, my effort had scarcely set the heather on fire. During question time, one of the ladies called out: 'Can Mr Maitland tell us why so many Scotsmen have spent their lives travelling abroad?' Before I could reply, Mrs MacDonald intercepted, 'Because they can't stand living in their own country!' Shrieks of laughter echoed round the hall.

This was the sort of lightning riposte the audience expected and adored. From then on, they and Mrs MacDonald were in their element. She described, with a totally deadpan expression, a Nile cruise which she and Jock had made shortly before the War. (By this time, any connections between Mrs MacDonald's summing-up address and my lecture were tenuous in the extreme.) She continued: 'A smelly old man in a ragged nightshirt sidled up and offered me a cup of filthy water he'd dredged from the Nile. "Drink this, lady", he said, "and you will surely return to Egypt." I replied, "If I drink that stuff, I'll never leave the place!" '

The *pièce de résistance* was a story about driving across France to Italy with one of her cousins, who like Mrs MacDonald had lived in India for many years. Neither of them spoke French. Neither, to quote Mrs MacDonald, 'had any sense of direction whatsoever'. Touring maps were double-Dutch to them. Perhaps I should add that all this took place long before the days of motorways, when

Continental travel was still something of an adventure. Mrs MacDonald paused. 'How did we manage, you enquire? Pretty rotten badly, I can tell you! Every few miles we had to stop and ask directions. I hailed everyone – man, woman and child – as ''Monsieur'' and then my cousin opened fire in Hindustani. It was catastrophic! We motored round and round in circles all over the place. Getting from Calais to Rome took us nearly a month. My husband said he thought we'd been carried off by white slave-traders. As a matter of fact, he was rather disappointed that we hadn't!'

When the laughter had died down, Mrs MacDonald turned to me and grinned. 'Now that was quite painless, wasn't it?' she said. 'At least they stayed awake. The chap we had the other day seemed to be an expert at mass-hypnosis. We could have made a fortune selling tape-recordings of his lecture. They'd have been a miracle cure for insomnia.'

My wanderings about Skye occasionally led me to Dunvegan Castle, the ancestral home of the MacLeods. I always enjoyed these visits. Dame Flora MacLeod, who was by then well into her eighties, and her daughter, Joan Wolrige-Gordon, were hospitable and very informative. They had been kind to me already, most of all by introducing me to Elizabeth Wakefield, whose cottage under Sgurr nan Gillean I tenanted for five years from autumn until the spring.

Dame Flora took an interest in my first efforts as a writer and artist and gave me a great deal of encouragement. She was companionable and friendly and made everyone who visited Dunvegan feel immediately at home. I remember one day at lunch, when the conversation turned to radio and television and, in particular, the role of the interviewer. 'I cannot understand why these people who question the politicians are so clumsy,' Dame Flora remarked. 'When I was a girl [she pronounced the word emphatically to rhyme with bell], we were taught how to put people at their ease.' She was a contemporary woman who prided herself in keeping abreast of current affairs. And yet, watching her small figure moving about the castle corridors, white-haired, her cheeks lightly powdered, in her flowing plaid skirt of dark-green

MacLeod tartan, she appeared more like the survivor of a bygone age.

Whenever I visited Dunvegan, my thoughts turned inevitably to Boswell and Johnson and the passage in Boswell's Hebridean Journal where he wrote: 'It was wonderful how well time passed in a remote castle, and in dreary weather'. Boswell gave a more detailed account of Dunvegan and its picturesque surroundings: 'The great size of the castle which is partly old and partly new, and is built upon a rock close to the sea, while the land around it presents nothing but wild, moorish, hilly and craggy appearances,' he wrote, 'gave a rude magnificence to the scene'. Boswell's brief sketch of Lady MacLeod, the laird's mother, might have applied equally well to Dame Flora two centuries later: 'We found the lady of the house a very polite and sensible woman', he observed, 'who had lived for some time in London ...'

Dame Flora was born on 3 February 1878. She was one of a large family, large even by Victorian standards. Her father, Sir Reginald MacLeod of MacLeod, from whom she inherited the clan chieftancy, was then Chancellor of the Exchequer and they lived at Number 11 Downing Street. However, as the family expanded, the Prime Minister, W.E. Gladstone, who was a bachelor, suggested that they move next door to Number 10, which was much more spacious, while he in turn removed to Number 11. In 1901 she married Hubert Walter, and thereafter her life was divided more or less between London and Dunvegan.

The MacLeods, who had formerly been staunch Jacobites, became unpopular in the early eighteenth century, when Norman MacLeod and Sir Alexander MacDonald of Sleat, Skye's two most powerful clan chiefs, refused to back Prince Charles Edward Stuart in the 1745 rebellion. MacLeod's treachery was not the only reason for his becoming hated and mistrusted by the islanders. It has been suggested that MacLeod and MacDonald failed to support the Prince for fear that the Navy might attack the exposed coastline of their estates. However, in a recently published history of Jacobitism, the author, Dr Frank McLynn, alleges that the reason for the chiefs' defection was less straightforward. In 1739, it appears that MacLeod and his kinsman, Sir Alexander MacDonald, had planned to profit by deporting numbers of their tenants to work side by side with slaves in the Southern plantations of America. None of these tenants nor their families had committed crimes punishable by transportation. When details of the sordid affair leaked out, MacLeod and MacDonald faced the threat of prosecution. By pledging their support for the Lord President Duncan Forbes's anti-Jacobite policies in the Highlands, MacLeod and MacDonald avoided being brought to trial.

Had Prince Charles Edward Stuart's army been reinforced by the MacLeod and MacDonald clansmen, he might have invaded England without confronting Cope at Prestonpans and successfully overthrown the Hanoverian regime. The ultimate defeat and humiliation of Culloden would never have occurred and the course of British history would have been drastically altered.

In the Highlands, especially in the Isles, where more than elsewhere the oral tradition kept the past alive, centuries-old events were discussed and pondered as if they had occurred only recently. The horrors of Norman MacLeod's transportation scheme were still fresh in people's minds when Dame Flora first set foot on Skye. The MacDonalds of Sleat had been equally unpopular, yet over the years they seemed to have weathered the scandal more successfully.

I have heard it said repeatedly that Dame Flora herself achieved far greater popularity abroad, for example in the United States and Canada, than she ever did on Skye where her overseas missions were to some extent misunderstood. Whenever I enquired about her, I was told, 'Oh, Dame Flora will most likely be away in America. She is forever going to America.'

Nevertheless, it must be admitted that few clan chiefs in modern times have been such tirelessly dedicated promoters of clan identity and the romance and mythology of clansmanship. National pride seldom flourishes more strongly than it does among expatriates. Dame Flora's widely publicised campaigns were directed mainly at expatriate MacLeods the world over, and there is no denying that they were outstandingly successful. Yet, at home in Dunvegan, she seemed curiously distanced and – dare one say it – estranged from the local people and their lives.

As far as I know, Boswell and Johnson during their stay at Dunvegan steered clear of any reference to the transportation scandal of thirty years before; or the then more recent, painfully vexed Jacobite question. Instead, over a sumptuous dinner of venison and claret, they discussed Dr Cadogan's book on gout, which Dr Johnson, being an interested party, thought 'good in general, as recommending temperance and exercise, and cheerfulness'. This gave some light relief to a heated debate over the church's right to make women do penance for fornication. Johnson's opinion that 'Where single women are licentious, you rarely find faithful married women' was disputed by Boswell, who insisted that among Indians 'the distinction is strictly observed'. As usual, the great lexicographer's reply brought the discussion to an abrupt end. 'Nay, don't give us India,' he retorted. 'That puts me in mind of Montesquieu, who ... whenever he wants to support a strange opinion, he quotes you the practice of Japan or of some other distant country of which he knows nothing.'

Boswell and Johnson were shown the Fairy Flag, a piece of faded yellow silk, which I suspect looked just as un-supernatural in 1773 as it does today.

Near Dunvegan there is a tiny island, not much bigger than a good-sized cottage garden, a flat strip of grass and rock which lies perhaps a hundred yards from the shore.

At low tide on a fine day I used to wade through the clear water to the island over a smooth bed of sand strewn with pink and white seashells. It always reminded me of a holiday we spent on Bute when I was a small boy. That year my father gave me a plastic model liner which had a transparent brown hull, green decks and green funnels. It was too unstable to float in the sea, and I sailed it instead in the rock-pools. The rocks, green and slimy with moss and algae, and the tidal pools with crabs and shells in them became the South Sea islands and lagoons I had read about in Ballantyne's adventure books for boys.

The island off the Dunvegan shore was a place for warm, windless afternoons. A place for lying on one's back in the sunshine and doing nothing. I have never seen primroses so large or so yellow as the primroses which flowered there every spring. They came out weeks before the rest because of the mild Gulf Stream climate, and they blossomed in hundreds. The warm green grass dotted with yellow primroses, the azure sea tinted pale orange near the shore, the sparkle of sunlight on the waves, the sun's dazzling reflection at the horizon and towers of soft blue cloud that rose out of the sea and stretched to infinity – all these I remember. And the good feeling of spring weather, after the drenching dark autumns, the winter mists and the weeks of unbroken grey skies.

Sometimes I tramped the sea-cliffs round Tallisker, on the west coast of Skye, where the boulders of black basalt, speckled white like a guinea-fowl's plumage, contained fragments of pink quartz which could be broken out with a small geological hammer. Sometimes I climbed in the Cuillins. The weather among the hills was unpredictable and could make rock-climbing dangerous. I usually climbed with friends who were expert mountaineers and very patient, for I was never more than a passenger, with little aptitude for the sport. I was often nervous and occasionally scared, but the mountain atmosphere had a strong appeal which overcame fear and drew me again and again to the high tops. This fascination never waned and in recent years, wandering about the Central Highlands and Argyll, the call of the great peaks has proved as irresistible as ever.

Even hill-walking in Skye was not without its moments of risk. Once on Marsco, in Glen Sligachan, I was scrambling over the east flank of the hill with a young housemaster from a famous English public school when the narrow path we were following suddenly petered out and left us stranded on a slippery grass slope which dropped away several hundred feet at an angle of 60 degrees. I was suddenly overcome by vertigo and felt myself being dragged off the hill as if by a huge magnet. I had never experienced vertigo before. I sat down on my heels, clinging to a tussock like grim death, turning down my toes inside my climbing boots as I felt them begin to slide away inch by inch under me. The danger, I am convinced, was more imagined than real; but the sensation was real enough and thoroughly unpleasant and for a while I could not bring myself to move. My companion remained where he was, leaning back into the hill a few feet ahead of me. I remember him saying, 'Try to concentrate on something. Don't look down. Try to think of something else.' I managed to get hold of a camera which was slung under my knapsack and took a photograph, hardly daring to look into the viewfinder. This did the trick. I got up and began to edge backwards a step at a time along the hill. It was difficult at first getting one foot behind the other, heel to toe, toe to heel. But then the ribbon of path appeared, we were safe and the rest of the afternoon went off without further incident.

Compared to the experiences of a real mountaineer, this adventure must seem trivial and hardly worth mentioning. Nevertheless, I know that a fall from that place would have been serious and I was relieved when we reached the gentle lower slopes. When I looked up and saw where we had come from, the incline, which from above appeared so frighteningly sheer, seen from the low ground lost all its terrors and looked like any other slope – the kind people fancy they can walk up in a few minutes. And that made me think.

Even in calm settled weather without a cloud in sight and not a breath of wind, it is better not to attempt the hills alone. Some years ago, one of the hotel guests left Sligachan on his own and set off for a day's tramping without telling anyone where he was going or when he expected to return. His remains were found a long time afterwards by a crofter who noticed the sun glinting on a bright object and went to investigate. It was the man's gold watch attached to its chain. It seems strange that he was never found at the time. The body was lying right out on the open moor, in Glen Sligachan. There was very little left of him. What happened remains a mystery, but the owner of Sligachan Hotel, Ian Campbell, told me that the man had probably died of heart-failure. There were no bones broken, and he was found some distance from Eagle's Rock, the only high ground in the vicinity.

I left Skye and Allt Dearg and Sebastian with mixed feelings of regret and accomplishment. I had made the effort and returned to the island, an experience which had been far easier than I had imagined. It had been a short stay, but a happy one.

It was good to see the Cuillins and other places which meant something. And it was good to smell the sea and the rain-soaked moors and listen again to the wind and the gulls' cries as they mobbed the ferry. Above all, it was good to feel the island all round me, as I used to, when I came back each winter knowing that I could settle for a time in surroundings where I found contentment.

For all that, my room at my parents' house near Blair Atholl, to which I now returned, seemed like a haven. I wrote up my notes there in peace and quiet, screened from the world by a line of chestnut trees; and then I planned what to do and where to go that spring and summer.

What I lacked in the way of money or possessions I made up for with health and strength, a sense of freedom and strong legs which carried me into the silent places which I believe with all my heart to be the real treasure in life. The Buddhist says that the world is sorrow, and that inner peace and understanding – which, to the Buddhist, are indivisible – come from enlightenment, from finding the true meaning of existence within oneself, without greed or ambition, or the desire for material things. This I agree with unreservedly; and yet, there is so much beauty, so much simple enjoyment in being alone among mountains where the wilderness of moor spreads all around you.

In a way, Skye had been a glimpse of Paradise. The morning by the Allt Dearg burn, when I sat watching the swifts above the cottage and the glittering, clear brown water. Or the days spent high up among the Cuillin Hills, or tramping the island's western shore.

But away from Skye, in my room at home, full of books and pictures and old photographs, I wondered seriously whether the *dream* of Paradise is not a better thing. The tramping man is a free-wheeler. His life is one of perpetual movement and discovery. His dreams are dreamed by the roadside, and the demands upon his time are what he alone chooses to make them. The world owes the tramp nothing; and his debts are those of foolishness and improvidence, or like the unremembered conversations which friends call up in repayment of the long overdraft of years. These are not things to be squared off and forgotten, but are markers, like the stepping-stones of youth which give life meaning and perspective.

Sebastian came to supper in London that September. I read him my notes and afterwards asked him whether they seemed like a true picture of what we had discussed and done together. He said that I'd got some of the details wildly wrong; but we agreed that it is virtually impossible to recreate a fixed image of experiences, or at any rate, one that tells a complete story. His view and mine were personal and different, however much we had found in common.

'Besides,' I said, 'I'm not trying to make a documentary of hard realities, I am trying only to impart something of the care-free, open-air life which so few experience and which many of us — especially those tied by strings of family responsibility, or a spirit of enterprise, or material ambitions, or ill-health — see as a way of escape. These things need saying, even in the pages of a book written by an unrepentant vagabond whose "whole business", like Frank Cassilis in Stevenson's *The Pavilion on the Links*, is to find "desolate corners".'

It was interesting to meet Sebastian in London. We had much the same sort of conversation as before. That evening, we shared the same sort of meal. Sebastian had cut his hair and arrived conventionally dressed in a laundered white shirt and tie. We sat in the drawing-room of my Chelsea flat with the windows wide open, for London was sultry and oppressive after a day of 75 degrees in the shade. Instead of the sea wind, we heard the low, insistent rumble of traffic and occasionally the whine of a jet coming over on the flight-path to Heathrow.

Sebastian had found his way by then. He had finally revoked the priesthood, and planned to train as a male nurse in a hospital south of the river. He said that his life had a definite direction at last, and I was glad. My wife, who like Sebastian is a Roman Catholic, also felt that he had made the right decision. Sebastian told me how much the weeks on Skye had meant to him, and how he still felt a longing to return some day to the island.

When we met, I was writing a review of a new book by a friend who had travelled 100,000 miles in countries so remote and wild that the wilds of Scotland seemed almost suburban by comparison. This man admitted that he avoided being alone whenever possible. His travels were important to him, not so much for the landscape or animals or the thrill of desert and lonely mountain terrain, but for the companionship he had found there.

'And still, you are not like him,' said Sebastian. 'You are for the solitary way, and the way of silent places.'

So the following year, I began a long summer's tramping through the Perthshire hills and glens, keeping a diary of the days and jotting down memories of other long walks and explorations I had made.

There was the reassurance of being in a familiar country I loved, which still held the promise of new sights and new adventures, and the lovely shock of surprise when the moorland renewed itself on fine days, clothing itself in an endless variety of delicate colours. There was much that I hadn't yet seen. New paths, unknown paths – what Spaniards call so evocatively *sendas incognitas* – to explore. Places where insignificant, deeply personal discoveries would be made; each in turn a step along the way which I would remember in the future with intense pleasure.

8 July 1986

The overnight coach from London has just drawn up in Pitlochry's main square. It's a glorious July morning – sunshine, blue sky and a lovely fresh breeze blowing.

On the way north I've been reading Stephen Graham's *Tramping with a Poet in the Rockies*. That was 1921 and this is 1986, but the message is the same. 'Well, it's good to be going tramping again', is Graham's opening sentence. He is right. It *is* good! I am off tramping for six weeks in the Atholl Forest. I'll follow the deer to the high tops. I'll sleep in a ditch under the stars. Whatever the weather, it's sunshine for me all the way!

The other day I had a letter from an old friend telling me that he had been to dinner with royalty. A footman in blue and gold livery served his food, another poured his wine, while a third fetched away his empty plate. My friend dined off exquisite porcelain and drank the finest claret from cut-crystal glasses. He said that everything was wonderful, but totally unreal.

Among the hills I'll dine off a tin plate with my fingers. I'll drink clear, cold water from a tin mug, and, when I've done, I'll wash my plate and mug in the river and then lie dreaming in the sun. This is real, and I say the real way is better.

The bus-driver fishes our baggage out of the hold with a long crooked pole. He dumps down a huge backpack, bursting at the seams, and grimaces good-naturedly at its owner, a tanned American college boy.

'Son,' says the driver, 'you must have the kitchen sink in here.' The boy points at his girlfriend's pack, which is even heavier than his own. He answers, 'No sir, the sink's in that one.'

Across the street, the greengrocer is busy outside his shop door setting up boxes of cabbages and cauliflowers and ripe red tomatoes. Already the local housewives are out in their billowy cotton frocks, and there are old men in rumpled tweeds gathered at the street corner, watching the passers-by. The summer weather has made everyone light-hearted. The little town is fairly buzzing with life and good humour. Everyone is on the sunny side of the street this morning, and everyone is making the most of it.

Unlike the young Americans, I have very little luggage. A small khaki ex-army haversack contains a couple of shirts, a jersey and two pairs of thick woollen socks. I've packed a sketchbook and a box of coloured crayons. The sleeves of my old tweed jacket have been mended with leather patches. My boots cost seven pounds and I'll walk them to destruction.

The big outdoor-clothing shops will tell you differently, but the fact is you can make do with far less than you imagine. There is a good deal of truth in the advice someone gave me years ago: pack two cases, a small one with the bare essentials and a larger one with the things you think you might need. Take the small case and leave the other one at home. The American students are a jolly pair, but like snails they carry their house on their shoulders.

'You've brought the good weather,' says the coach driver. When I tease him and say, 'Why don't you come too?' he chuckles defensively. The driver is a big stout man who looks forward to his three square meals a day and his dram of whisky in the evening. He has the Highlander's roving blue eyes, but his soul is rooted in *terra firma*.

'Walking's too much like hard work,' he replies.

My parents live about a mile from Blair Atholl, which in turn lies
seven miles north of Pitlochry on the main road to Inverness. They
have a house built of grey sandstone, with 'crow-stepped' gables.
The house looks out over Tulach Hill and the garden is screened by
a small plantation of firs, with a line of tall chestnut trees on the far
side. I made my base here for most of the summer.

Looking through my diary, I see that it rained every day for
thirty-seven days out of forty. There were three brilliantly clear
sunny days when the weather got really warm and the temperature
rose above 80 degrees in sheltered spots out of the wind. These fine
days made up for others when it poured and blew and sleeted.

The great thing is to take what comes and make the best of it. I
did so, and enjoyed every minute.

My notebooks tell what happened from day to day and give a
patchwork impression of what it was like to be always on the move,
tramping sometimes for twelve or fourteen hours on end, or else

idling the hours away basking in the warm sun on a hillside deep in purple heather. I have left these notes very much as they were first written. They are very much like the sketches I made as I went along, which, to me, are worth infinitely more than the careful work I did in the studio months afterwards.

When you are off alone among the hills, as everybody knows your thoughts stray continually from the surroundings. For this reason my notes cut backwards and forwards in time. The plain record of days is interleaved with memories of the twenty years I have tramped in the Perthshire glens.

My mother and father were wonderfully patient and considerate and did all they could, and more, to make life carefree. When I returned home, tired, exhilarated and usually starving, they fed me and listened to my stories and then left me to my own devices, with ample peace and quiet to write up my notes and finish the rough open-air sketches which had had to be abandoned all too frequently because of the weather. There is no substitute for sketching out of doors; but Scotland is not like Spain or Provence where you wake up to marvellous sunshine and blue skies one day after another.

Rain is death to watercolours. There is very little shelter in our sort of country and broken, showery weather gives little or no opportunity for working on large sheets in big colour-washes which take time to dry. Instead I used small sketchpads and crayons which could be packed and unpacked very rapidly. I suppose I should have brought a camera, but I didn't and I do not regret it. Once my mother allowed me to borrow her Box Brownie, and I took a few snapshots which I redrew later. But these sketches made from photographs failed to satisfy me. The colours were accurate and they recorded the light and shadow with great precision, but somehow they ended up too contrived and too mechanically perfect. Working up the crayon sketches achieved better results, possibly because I relied more on memory than the exact visual record.

The memory method, I have always found, keeps alive feelings which I have experienced at the time, in a way a photograph never quite manages to do. Someone who remarked that I was foolish to ignore the camera's advantages – he meant its ability to freeze the changes of light, or a moving shadow which came and went in a few seconds – seemed to me to have missed the point entirely.

Simply because the light *does* change so rapidly and continuously in the hills, the final rendering of a scene makes very little difference.

Few of my sketches show exactly what I saw at a given moment, any more than my attempts to reproduce snatches of conversation are word-perfect. None of this matters in the slightest. The impression is the great thing. And the impression is what lasts.

9 July

On the first day out, I met a doctor halfway along Glen Tilt. She was a perfect advertisement for her profession, tremendously fit and healthy-looking with a golden tan and sun-bleached brown hair cropped short. She told me that her ambition was to climb all the Munros. These are Scottish peaks which rise to 3,000 feet and over, and there are 277 of them! She would need to be brave and very determined, but the doctor was all these things, and what is more, she painted in watercolours. She laughed heartily when I remarked that tramping and sketching makes a good life, but a poor living.

A man who conquered all the Munros in a single winter has written a book about his experiences. He completed what a reviewer described as 'his monstrous obstacle race' in eighty-three days of 'bruising confrontation with hurricanes, rain, sleet, sub-zero temperatures and darkness'. Without a doubt, his achievement was admirable, but as far as I am concerned, I have no desire to compete with nature. I have come here to the hills seeking peace of mind and the sense of exhilaration which deepens and intensifies as you go, step by step, higher and higher, until there is nothing but the sky, the bare rock and the landscape far beneath spreading to infinity.

The truth is, I am more of a hill-pantheist than a mountaineer. I lack the mountaineer's urge to conquer what is there; and yet, I share his love for space and silence. Even more, I love the romance of the hills. My imagination peoples them with demons, witches and the wraiths of clansmen and free-foresters of a bygone age. I love the challenge of a rock-face when uncertainty and a twinge of fear sharpen the wits, but I have no wish to conquer a summit for its own sake. Far better to live among the mountains, to become part of them, to revel in the mountain solitude.

The track through the glen led to a shepherd's cottage surrounded by lush green meadows. The meadows were crowded with sheep and lambs. Long before I saw them, I heard their noisy bleating which carried for a considerable distance. In a fenced paddock near the cottage, about a dozen men in blue overalls were hard at work shearing the ewes. I sat down at the edge of the track and sketched them until, after about an hour, the men downed tools and filed into a long clapboarded shed for the midday meal.

While I was sketching, I noticed a shepherd and two black and white collies driving a small flock of sheep down from the hill. The dogs worked as a team. Sometimes they made short rushes, belly to the ground; sometimes they circled the flock at a loose trot like timber-wolves. The man above appeared to operate them by remote-control. There was a good deal of 'ho-ho-ho-ing' and 'aye-aye-ing' and I learned afterwards that, as a rule, the hill shepherds only whistle when the dogs are too far away for voice commands to reach them.

One of the shepherds explained the technique of shearing. The shearer pulls up a ewe by her front legs and grips her between his knees. The first cut or 'blow' is made at the neck, under the chin, and the second cut opens up the belly fleece. (The fleece is, of course, solid.) The sheep is held with her head under the shearer's left arm, with her back legs under the man's right leg. Long sweeping cuts are made from the sheep's tail to its neck. Usually eight or ten sweeps are enough to remove the fleece. The last sweeps are made with the ewe turned belly-uppermost.

The electric clipper works like ordinary hair-clippers. A blade

standing fully clothed in a shower. The creamy brown torrent below me was aptly named in Gaelic *Allt Féith nam Fearne*: in rough translation, 'stream of the pass through boggy ground where alders grow'.

The sun broke through and the bleak, sodden moorland was instantly transformed. I opened my flannel shirt to the waist and let it blow dry in the breeze. I followed the Allt Féith nam Fearne to its confluence with the Banvie and then struck out across a lush water-meadow, like an amphitheatre gouged out from the hillside with high grassy bankings on three sides. The grass was littered with bones and the bleached white skulls of sheep and deer. At a bend in the stream I found the rotting carcass of a stag, its forelegs and antlers wedged between some large boulders. Shreds of transparent skin and guts drifted waveringly in the current. The tattered remains looked like an umbrella blown inside-out. It was a pathetic sight, although by no means an uncommon one.

I sat in the sun and sketched the stag until the flies got too
bothersome. Far away at the skyline, a herd of sixty stags cantered
in slow procession out of a pine wood where Glen Banvie joins Glen
Bruar. Their colours varied from pale oatmeal to dark brown. Some
were in velvet; others, as stalkers say, were already 'in the hard'.
The stags made a fine picture, strung out across the sunlit moor with
a curtain of dark blue cloud behind them.

From the pine wood came the faint buzzing of petrol-driven
chainsaws, where some woodmen were trimming the piles of newly
felled timber.

Tramping the high moorland towards Bruar, I got three more
drenchings which did not matter except for a cold wind now
blowing from the north, made colder still by my clinging damp shirt
and trousers. The Bruar river was low, and when the sky cleared it
looked very lovely patched with blue and white reflections. I lay
face-down and drank where the water ran down hard between the
stones, getting wet in the process; but I was already too wet to care.

11 July

This morning I took the south track through Glen Banvie. I followed a small party of hikers as far as the plantation. Their pace exactly matched my own and, short of breaking into a run, there was no hope of overtaking them.

It was dry and mild with very little wind, and an occasional blink of watery sunshine. A thick layer of dust covering the track whitened my boots and reminded me of good times past, tramping the byways of Provence and northern Spain.

After a time, the constantly bobbing back view of the hikers began to irritate me. I threw down my knapsack and stretched out full-length in the grass just off the track. When the hikers had disappeared into the wood, I went down to the Allt Féith nam Fearne and finished off the previous day's sketch of the dead stag, which lay sprawled in mid-stream just as I had left it.

12 July

After breakfast I spent an hour in Pitlochry buying groceries and other odds and ends. In the afternoon I walked over Glen Tilt by way of Tirinie.

The cottages at Tirinie line the roadside up a steep hill beyond the bridge. They have slate roofs and grey stone walls and white-painted doors and windows. There are wire-mesh flower baskets hanging from the eaves and trim herbaceous borders ablaze with marigolds, nasturtiums, delphiniums and pansies. Some of the cottages have a trellis of pink or red roses round the door. A burn overhung by shady planes and chestnuts divides the hamlet, and its murmurous plashing can be heard everywhere.

Tirinie is a haven of tranquillity. Even Pitlochry seems overcrowded and noisy by comparison. Time means nothing here. Life, like the stream, flows along at its own pace. Nobody hurries. There is nothing to hurry for.

In Glen Tilt, I caught up with some girls who were marching five-abreast down a fire-track. They held their ground and ignored me as I edged past them. When I remarked cheerily, 'This is a bit like Oxford Street', one of the girls, a freckled, lanky teenager with rimless spectacles and a shock of carrotty-red hair snapped back: 'We are hill walkers, and hill walkers are solitary people'. Her reprimand baffled me for a while. In the end, however, I decided that she meant I should have pushed on without uttering a word, as though neither she nor I existed.

The same girl had been telling her companions about 'a tiny wee island' in the Kyles of Bute where she had stayed for a week with a schools' ecology group. 'Of course, we couldn't go just where we liked,' she explained gravely. 'We had to keep within the parameters of our individual study zones.'

It seemed to me a pity that young minds should be broken to the specialised view and its jargon so early.

Later, as I tramped through the glen, I thought again about Tirinie and wondered what it might be like to live there, day in day out, all year round. As a place to come back to after long spells of wandering, it might be ideal. But then, the same could be said of a hundred other places – not least our small cottage on the Clyde. To find contentment in these out of the way corners, you must first of all be at peace with yourself. I'm a restless individual and, after a while, I find the routine of a settled life begins to pall. It is important for me always to have the prospect of another journey in view.

14 July

A ribbon footpath not much wider than my boots placed side by side forked north-west from the main Glen Tilt track over the high moors to Glen Bruar. First the path led through scrub woodland and then out into the heather. A burn to the right of the path splashed along its bed of mossy stones, falling in tiny clear cascades like a moving staircase through a series of calm brown pools. My friend the oyster-catcher was there, smartly turned out in his black and white morning suit, but it was his bright vermilion beak I noticed first. Tiny brown birds darted to and fro along the burn to drink and shower-bath at the water's edge. Butterflies attached themselves like paper flowers to the gently nodding stems of moorland grass.

There is nothing quite so attractive as the trail that disappears over the horizon. I feel immediately curious to discover what lies on the other side, and my pace quickens instinctively. Once, in Italy, that most eloquent of travellers, Freya Stark, challenged me to solve the following riddle which she'd invented. She asked: 'What is it that divides Mankind?' To her unconcealed delight, the puzzle defeated me. Her answer was this: 'Mankind is divided by the horizon. For some of us, the horizon suggests a safe enclosure. For others, it offers an irresistible invitation to adventure. It's as simple as that.' Tracks which vanish among woodland are interesting, but the moorland track has a special magnetism of its own.

The sun came out just as I got to the highest point of the moor where the hills rose a thousand feet on either side. Here, the track widened enough for a car to pass. The going became very rough. I scrambled over the great shards of orange and white sandstone and rocky splinters mixed with shale. The luminous atmosphere at the summit reminded me of the sea-light on the south coast of England. It seemed absurd to think of conservatories, potted palms and tea-time trios in that sort of country.

15 July

Cold and overcast at day-break. Warm and sunny as the day progressed.

I stood watching a crèche of baby rabbits playing in and out among the green ferns and long, dew-soaked grass, scurrying back and forth across the track. Whenever I moved, however slightly, several of them raced away at full speed, while others sat perfectly still, apparently convinced that they were invisible. One ran along the track towards me and stopped abruptly six feet away. It crouched there for a few seconds, twitching its nose, and then dived into the verge. The baby rabbits had yet to discover the art of camouflage. They would learn the hard way, for these woods are full of weasels and foxes, hawks, carrion crows, even the occasional eagle in search of a meal. The death toll among the innocents must be a large one.

It had rained during the night and the track was waterlogged and muddy where it passed under the field-gates. The woods smelled of wet bracken. Here and there I caught a nostalgic whiff of honeysuckle.

17 July

On the 16th I travelled to Glasgow and from there to Erskine Cottage where I spent the night with my uncle. The afternoon train arrived back at Pitlochry a little after 4 p.m. and I decided to walk from there to Blair Atholl taking the high road past Tenandry, a distance of about eight miles.

A strong headwind blowing from the north-west made the walk unexpectedly hard going. Once out of the wind near Tenandry, however, the air became humid and muggy, and as I climbed towards the church I found myself perspiring freely.

The last few miles, walking the verges of the A9 main road, were unpleasant. The A9 is the main route to Inverness and a continuous stream of cars and heavy lorries rushed past in both directions. A cross-country runner in an electric-blue vest and shorts brushed past me without warning. His sudden appearance startled me. The man loped grimly by, puffing and blowing in rhythmic gasps, red-faced, beaded and glistening with sweat. He was soon half a mile ahead, his lead increasing with every stride. The combination of speed and endurance impressed me. I'm fine when it comes to tramping long distances. Running them is something else.

I was glad to turn off the main road at last into the tree-lined drive leading to my parents' house near the castle. I made a mental note to avoid all main roads in future. Clearly the byways, not the highways, were the thing to aim at.

19 July

Today I visited a folly built on a hill top at the edge of a small wood. The weather had stayed very close and showery. The landscape was all greens and browns, fading to blue and purple in the distance, with a blanket of grey unbroken cloud above. The hill leading to the folly was wet and midgy. The building was little more than a shell, and the sheep which graze in and out among the ruins clattered away baaing loudly as I came in sight.

Near the folly I met a woodman from Deeside walking in the

spinney with his wife and children and their dog, a lovely brown and white Welsh spaniel. We talked for a long time about the various grades of timber in a forestry block where he had been felling on contract. The woodman was a cheerful man with big, calloused hands and a lined face which told years of hard labour. He said that he felt more at home among trees than he did in open country. He thought that natural woodland softened the Highland scene, but he disapproved strongly of the vast geometrical plantations of spruce and larch which dominated the skyline nearby.

Further on I saw a ewe which was on the point of giving birth. She stood bow-legged, panting, a balloon of shiny reddish-purple placenta protruding under her tail. All round her, other ewes lay in the wet grass chewing the cud. They paid no attention to her plight. Such is nature.

The air stung with the carbolic-green odour of pine and the acrid smoke from a cottage in the glen where an old man was busy tending a garden bonfire.

It began to rain heavily.

Two cyclists appeared through the driving wet. They were quite the clumsiest I have ever seen. Spanish students: one with his long black hair tied in a red headcloth like an Apache, his companion lean and swarthy with a crown of tight brown curls. Both men were caped in yellow plastic ponchos and they seemed far too large and long-limbed for their light machines. I had never before associated Spaniards with bicycles. All Spanish men ought surely to be straight-backed like the strutting Dresden statuettes of the bullring. Hunched up over the handlebars of a touring bike, they looked ridiculous. Put a Spanish bull on roller-skates and you have a picture of those two as they battled into the rain. Proud, pawing creatures reduced to an undignified shambles.

Coming down the hill, I found Donald, who looks after the trekking ponies and a gigantic, lumbering Clydesdale mare named 'Goldie'. Donald informed me that he had been breaking-in some

new ponies to harness. His skin was as brown and polished as the harness itself and the aroma of horses clung to him, like tobacco to a pipe-smoker. 'Patience is the great thing wi' horses,' said Donald. He had a gentle, hesitant smile and steady blue eyes. 'Same as wi' bairns, ye ken. Nae use having bairns if ye havna' patience.' Donald was hard of hearing and his voice, bursting out loudly like a West Highland minister preaching fire and brimstone, seemed out of keeping with his placid nature.

20 July

Breezy and sunny all day.

I tramped twenty-four miles beyond Bruar Lodge and back. At a ruined bothy called Ruiclachrie I met a hiker and his dog, a big fierce German Shepherd which he kept close by him on a heavy chain-link and leather lead. The hiker's name was Archie Johnston. He had been a merchant seaman for eleven years and was now a labourer, an artist and a tramping man.

Archie had dark eyes and an infrequent, shy smile. He talked to me about his life at sea, his 'wonderful wife' and his love of solitude and the great spaces of moor and hills. Yet despite being happily married, he nevertheless felt tied down. He felt hemmed in by responsibilities and longed to break free of them. He smiled: 'I just want to walk on and on, and never turn back.'

He told me that he had met the rambler Derek Wainwright in Keswick the year before. 'Funny thing,' said Archie, 'it was the only time I was ever in Keswick. I liked Mr Wainwright. He was an interesting man. But to start with, getting a word out of him was like drawing teeth.'

Archie had slept the previous night in the open. There had been high winds and heavy rain, but he didn't mind, and said that, after all, it was part of the outdoor life.

His sketches were simple and artless. A few showed promise. Archie was proud of some he'd made into postcards, which he sold in local restaurants and hotels; but he realised his limitations and said he wished he had had some training in art years ago. The navy had unsettled him — always on the move, always surrounded by the

limitless expanse of ocean. He pined for the open air, incarcerated in a small factory at Dundee, and he could hardly wait for weekends to come round. Sometimes his 'wonderful wife' joined him, but more often than not he went off by himself with his dog. Archie was the kind of person who looks you straight in the eye and seems to penetrate your most private thoughts. Yet he was far from being inquisitive. He was an eager conversationalist, but also what the French call *un homme fermé*. He shuffled and remarked how much he had enjoyed our talk and how unusual it was to find a kindred spirit, as it were, by chance. 'That'll make half a page in the diary,' he said, grinning. I made a quick sketch of him in my notebook and watched as he tramped away. Archie did not look back.

Further up, near the mountaineering hut, I passed two girls, one of them helping the other to adjust her backpack. They were very white-skinned and flush-faced. They had identical white windcheaters and microscopic red running shorts. They bemoaned the storm of the night before, 'an awful experience with the sky pressing down all round the hut' and the sheet rain and wind keeping them awake. The girls' view was a prosaic one: down-to-earth and dully practical.

A mile above Bruar Lodge, I sat down in the warm sun, pulled off my boots and socks and paddled my feet in a deliciously cold burn which flowed down from a waterfall halfway up the hillside. I walked barefoot over the soft springy turf strewn with buttercups and daisies and patches of pink bell-heather. I picked some tiny heliotrope flowers in order to identify them later. There were immense cloud-shadows chasing across the hills and the rush of the wind and the sound of water gushing from a dam further down the glen. The roar of the dam's outflow sounded just like the wind among the Banvie pine trees.

When I first saw the dam from a distance I had imagined I was looking at the front of a cottage undergoing repair. The dam's surface made the slate-grey roof and the sluices lined up below like three square windows, while the water tumbling down was for all the world like sheets of clear polythene flapping in the breeze. I was completely taken in until I got up closer, where the dam flashed up clear in front of me like a picture projected onto a screen.

This was a lovely day. I felt very relaxed and fit and more at home among the scenery. So far I have taken things easy. 140 miles in twelve days.

22 July

A long day tramping through Glen Tilt. I thought a lot about the weather and how one ought to make friends with the wind and rain as well as the sunshine. When you manage this, the whole business of tramping becomes much more fun. There are really no off-days after that.

I spied for trout off the parapet of a stone bridge, an attractive single-span affair built by General Wade. The trout, suspended in the dappled brown water, looked like miniature silver airships. The water varnished the ledged rocks and intensified their colours like polished gemstones.

A van parked among the trees had what at first glance appeared to be some naked men and girls sprawled on its roof. A foreign saloon beside the van bore the registration letters KI:LT. The nudes turned out to be tailor's dummies and the van, I saw, belonged to an Edinburgh school whose name was printed on the sides in graceful Trajan capitals. Later, the van bounced by in a shower of dust and stones. I called out to one of the boys inside it: 'What are the dummies for?'

He winked and yelled back, 'That'd be telling!'

I suspect they have something to do with an International Boy Scout Jamboree in the grounds of Blair Castle. About 700 boys from all over the world have assembled there, as well as a contingent of 150 Girl Guides. The Jamboree village consists of red, blue and orange tents of all shapes and sizes, with a giant white marquee in the middle. There are triangular flags from all nations strung on lines between the trees and some painted totem-poles.

Some young keepers and shepherds were busy filling in the potholes along the track leading to Forest Lodge. The first shooting-tenants must be expected soon, hence the sudden burst of activity.

I wrote up the last few days' notes sitting on a hillside in Glen Tilt overlooking Marble Lodge, where I used to live. A succession of

enormous cloud-shadows was followed by a thundering of hooves. A herd of Friesian cows galloped past within a few yards of me, the farmer strolling after them, shouting furious imprecations – 'Get on, ye stupid beasts!' and so on. When I bade him good-day, the farmer nodded disinterestedly and muttered, 'Aye', which is the standard, all-purpose greeting hereabouts.

The cattle and the farmer were followed in turn by a nervous-looking family: mother, father and two small children, with a terrier prancing excitedly on its lead. *Townspeople*. There was no mistaking them. The woman's low-heeled patent-leather shoes were clogged with manure and the man's knife-edge-creased beige slacks were mud-spattered. The woman looked as though she had seen a ghost.

More lovely cloud-effects over Tulach Hill. Dazzling white surf, breaking over lagoons of mottled indigo. The line of jagged hills beneath like blue Caribbean waves. The sky blanching from azure to pale lemon.

Among the ferny leaves growing on a stone wall near Old Blair, I found the tiniest wildflowers I have yet seen. In a wild cottage garden nearby, a stout woman in a green headscarf wandered about in the long grass, talking to her chickens and a little shaggy-coated cream and brown pony which stood with its chin resting on the fence.

23 July

Last night there was a full moon. Ragged black clouds, lined with ermine, floating by. The night sky reminded me of a wonderful description I had read of a schooner berthing at Tahiti – jasmine-scented darkness and bright harbour lights that twinkled in the water like fallen stars.

At day-break I walked up through a narrow glen where there were bluebells growing everywhere. The Scots bluebell, or harebell, is not really blue at all. Inside it is pale violet; a deeper shade of bluish-violet outside, with tiny specks of rust-red. We can scarcely describe the subtle colouring of these wildflowers unless, like the Germans, we string caravans of adjectives together. Yet in Polynesia they manage to convey something as complex as the sunset in a single word: coral-pink and vermilion, mauve and indigo, shot through with streamers of gold and green and orange. Everybody knows what you mean. They hear the word and they see the whole picture at once.

What changes the centuries have wrought throughout Scotland and yet, in the remote glens, how much remains unchanged. The wildflowers in their thousands, the hills, moorland, fishes in the burn, stones encrusted with grey lichen, old gaunt pines and the drifting patchwork sky.

The bothy which stands beside the Allt Sheicheachan burn is protected from the wind by an outcrop which unfortunately screens the view towards Schiehallion, 'the Fairy Hill of the Caledonians'. The rooms are swept and tidy with stone-flagged floors and a sleeping place under the rafters which you climb into by means of a light aluminium ladder.

The hut is maintained by the Mountain Bothies Association, but I was distressed to read in the visitors' book how in 1983 the wooden mantelpiece and some benches were smashed up for firewood by hill-walking parties who had spent the night there.

A couple from the north country turned up just as I was leaving. They had been caught in a tremendous downpour high up on Beinn Dearg, and they were soaked to the skin and chattering with cold. The woman's bare legs were red and shining. Her husband, dressed in white from top to toe, was as pale as a phantom. It made me shiver just to look at him.

The man stood and shook himself like a dog. 'God,' he groaned, 'what a bloody awful day! We've seen nowt but rain since last Friday. It's bucketed every bloody minute! How folks here put up with it, God knows!'

'But surely it rains nearly as much where you come from?' I said.

The man glowered. 'Aye, right enough it does. But that's *rain*. Here, it's like being at the bottom of the bloody ocean!'

I completed a rough sketch which I'd begun on the hill, and left the bothy just as the rain settled in for the rest of the day. The hills and moor looked lovely: planes of satin-grey and violet receding into the mist behind a heavy drizzle like gently waving net curtains, bleaching the colours. The steeper slopes were heavy-going by then. A case of one step forward and two back, the sprigs of heather like miniature watering-cans showering my legs with spray.

This is fine walking country, but great care must be taken by anyone who attempts the wilder parts in rough weather, especially if as I do they go alone.

25 July

The other day I found a book by an American naturalist called David Grayson. It was written not long after the First World War and its title is *Great Possessions*. Grayson described himself as one of the 'Green People' who love not merely the sight and scent but also the *taste* of trees and shrubs growing in the hedgerow. The idea of the 'Green People' intrigued me and I resolved to carry out some experiments.

First, I broke off a birch twig and – I have to admit, rather hesitantly – chewed it. The flavour was sweet and not unpleasant. Beech twigs, I found, tasted less sweet. Chestnut was mellow. To my surprise, the shoots of bramble and wild raspberry tasted bland and rather nondescript. But I am bound to agree with David Grayson, that by far the best was the bitter-sweet, woody, green flavour of pine. After trying a good many, my mouth was left with an astringent sensation, not unlike the after-effect of sucking a lemon, which I attributed to mixing the various species at random like some sort of arboreal cocktail.

A shepherd pedalling slowly by gave me a quaint, old-fashioned look. Who could blame him? My early morning browse among the foliage must have seemed very odd indeed.

Be that as it may, the long-forgotten New Englander had sparked off in me a fascinating new line of enquiry with infinite scope for experiment. It goes without saying, of course, that trees and shrubs of certain types must be avoided – for example, yew and laurel. I should perhaps add that, like any self-respecting wine-taster, I spat out each sappy mouthful and let the after-taste subside before sampling a different vintage.

The mileage is slowly building, but this by itself means nothing. What happens along the way is what matters. Here, in Perthshire, I would rather get to know a few glens thoroughly. I have never before in my life had so much leisure to accomplish this. Old haunts where I have tramped for fifteen years strike different chords every time. Nature mirrors nature in endless variety. There is also the matter of rediscovering oneself. Nothing I have done has been very original or daring. These days contain little or nothing of what might be termed high adventure. Variety is a fine thing, and even conquests such as climbing all the Munros have their own value, so long as we don't delude ourselves by thinking that they represent the last word in achievement. Rest ye not upon laurels. After all, where do you go next? What remains?

Some people say there is *nothing* new under the sun. Well, I say different. Get up with the new dawn! Watch the sun rise and see the world afresh. Time means nothing in nature. Every day a new door opens. If you see it like this, life is all revelation and adventure.

26 July

Going up Glen Banvie this morning, the rain blew hard across on a west wind. I used an old plastic sandwich-bag as a rain-hat and found it excellent, warm and dry. I have tramped well over 200 miles and have no blisters, thanks to woollen socks and boots which fit. I trudged along singing 'The Road to Mandalay'. Orwell was absolutely right when he said that these verses are among Kipling's finest things.

All the time, the hills were changing: bright and then sombre strong lights overlaid and muted with a succession of dark shadows. A painter told me the other day: 'Never think of shadow as a separate colour. Shadow is merely a glaze with the colour coming through. Look at something through a pair of sunglasses and you'll see immediately what I'm getting at.' I did so, and the penny dropped.

Near the keeper's cottage I witnessed a grisly spectacle: sawn-off hooves dumped in galvanised pails and flayed carcasses of deer hanging from steel hooks, blue and red-raw, reeking death.

I discovered afterwards that at that moment my mother had been in our village church arranging the flowers for the Sunday service.

27 July

I wasted the morning making a drawing of a stag and hinds in watercolours. This theme has been done to death and no matter how I try to vary the attitudes and background, there is an awful, deadly repetition in the work which has begun to bore me. Some people go on painting deer very successfully, so the fault must be mine, I suppose.

Near Gilbert's Bridge in Glen Tilt, where I spent the remainder of the day, a sparrow-hawk came out, circling slowly over the trees. Suddenly I heard screams and the hawk's angry mewing and I saw the hawk and a seagull attacking each other like enemy fighter-planes. Eventually the gull chased the hawk away, giving vent to a series of triumphant cries as it made its victory circuit overhead.

On the way back, in the arboretum near the castle, I came across a party of women standing beside an enormous Japanese larch. Its girth at the base was over nine feet, and it stood 130 feet high. I knew the tree well. Sometimes, on a good day, I would sit facing the sun with my back to the tree and read a book, while in the branches high above me a crossbill picked at the larch's winged, resinous seeds which are his favourite food.

The larch's botanical name, *Laxis kaempferi*, totally baffled the onlookers. 'Kaempferi,' said one, 'that sounds just like Broughty Ferry!' They all burst out laughing.

Poking fun at the strange label was their way of coming to terms with the unknown. The joke cleared away its mysteries. Even so, it seemed odd to find people laughing at a tree.

28 July

Cloudy and humid again, with the usual squadrons of flies and midges in pursuit. The insect-repellent I bought in London was not 100 per cent effective unless you spread it on like butter. At Loch Moraig on the way to Glen Fender the breeze carried glorious smells of new-mown grass.

Far away across the fields to my left, I saw a roebuck feeding in some long grass thickly sown with buttercups. As soon as I appeared, the shy creature bounded away. A few minutes later, it came rushing back and crossed the road at the edge of a fenced plantation of Sitka spruce. The roe could neither jump the high fence nor find a way through the fine wire-mesh stretched between the posts. It became quite frantic and tore backwards and forwards, searching desperately for a way in or over. Each time it stopped, seventy or eighty yards away, to stare at me. Then it whipped round and bounded out of sight. The performance was repeated several times. On its last mad race, the roebuck crashed head-first into a wooden fence-post. It sprang into the air, badly alarmed, its wits scattered, and then dashed off across the buttercup field where it disappeared for good.

The animal's resistance to the blow astonished me. A human would have been brained, or at the very least knocked unconscious.

Near Loch Moraig I found a party of Scouts, six small boys weighed down with backpacks, negotiating a five-barred gate. The gate was padlocked and the youngest boy was having a tremendous job heaving himself over. His face was scarlet – 'like a harvest moon', as my grandmother used to say – and shining with sweat. 'It's this bloomin' pack!' he gasped. 'Come on, you lot! Gie's a hand up!'

He got little sympathy from his mates, a hardy good-natured crowd, a mixture of Scots and Germans and Geordies from Newcastle. The little chap's long-legged baggy shorts reminded me of Richmal Crompton's *Just William*. When he got his breath back he explained that they were bound for the River Tilt. 'We'll take our bearings just here,' he said, jabbing his map with a grimy forefinger. 'That'll get us to the river, no bother.' I hadn't the heart to tell him that the Tilt was less than a mile away at the bottom of the hill. He was so serious about the whole affair, and anyhow, I reflected, compass-training was useful.

They set off again and I slouched about watching the moorhens and seagulls on the loch. A little later, a blue Land Rover swept past, caught up with the wayfarers and carried them off to one of the camping areas further down the glen.

The main Jamboree camp looked more and more like a Red Indian settlement with the 'braves' whooping and racing madly in all directions. The Girl Guide squaws looked on disdainfully. One remarked to a companion: 'Look at them, running about like little boys!'

The companion answered: 'But they *are* little boys.'

The other pulled a face and muttered, 'Oh well – you know what I mean.'

29 July

In Glen Banvie I got within five or six yards of a young hare. It lolloped away and sat bolt upright for several minutes just off the track. When I moved closer, the hare laid its ears flat along its back, shot away in a big circle and vanished into a ditch a hundred yards further along. I sat on a hillock and watched the grass blowing in the breeze and the sun shining on the bent stalks. The heather was coming into bloom and there were patches of purple where there had been great slashes of brown across the green hillside. I saw a dragonfly – the first this year. I remembered the dragonflies I saw three years ago in some marshy ground in Argyllshire. Electric-blue, whirring by like miniature helicopters. I have never seen so many in one place.

30 July

This morning I rose before 7 a.m. and tramped through Glen Tilt for twelve miles and then back by way of Tirinie and the village. Near Kincraigie the shepherd was driving in a flock of about seventy sheep. We passed the time of day and he asked if I would mind acting as a 'stop' while he got the sheep past a fork in the farm-track into their pen. It was sheer delight to see the man and his two dogs working them round. The shepherd spoke with a cultured voice. His ragged jumper with both elbows out and his old corduroys and gumboots gave the impression of a Buchan character, a dropout and a gentleman living the life he chose. He would have been perfectly as ease in any sort of company.

We went our separate ways, but we could have found any amount to talk about. However, the shepherd was a working man and had little enough time to spare for idle gossip with a vagabond such as myself.

Just as the rain started I found a strange fungus attached to a tree stump, which I kicked off and dropped into my plastic collecting-bag. The fungus was jet-black and looked like an old-fashioned spinning-top.

In Glen Tilt, a mile from Marble Lodge, a couple were fishing off the rocks. The woman sat on a big ledge overhanging the water, hunched up, bored-looking, with her rod tucked under her arm. Her fair ponytail stuck straight out from under a brand-new green waterproof hat. She and her husband had identical green jackets and green wellingtons. Their clothes and tackle looked new and unfamiliar.

I called out: 'What's the fishing like?'

The man replied, 'No luck so far.'

His reply to 'What are you using?' was repeated again and again, and lost in the loud rush of water. It sounded like 'crow bait'. The eddying north wind and the rough water made accurate casting well-nigh impossible. It wasn't that sort of fishing anyhow.

The members of an all-male hiking club shouldered past without so much as a word. They did not even talk to each other. None had eyes for anything save the road. Perhaps they were Trappists? I felt curiously disembodied, like a will-o'-the-wisp. And then I remembered somebody in London who went about in an old cardigan full of holes, and a friend saying: 'But dear Agnes thinks she is invisible.'

31 July

A night spent at home in a comfortable bed with my books about me. Sheer bliss! During the night it rained heavily, and I woke to grey skies and drizzle.

Today I made a seven-mile tramp from Pitlochry to Kinnaird Cottage where Robert Louis Stevenson wrote *Thrawn Janet* and *The Body Snatchers*. The walk was nothing, but the journey was everything. My American cousins in San Rafael would call it 'a pilgrimage'. They are right, of course; it was a pilgrimage. Every bit as much as one we have just made to Lourdes, or Belloc's tremendous walk to Rome. It's all relative.

The post-bus collected me at the road-end at 12.30 sharp. The post-bus was really a small family saloon. The postman got out and opened the back door and ushered me in as politely as any doorman at Claridges or the Ritz. I squeezed up knee-to-knee with an elderly lady travelling from Calvine, a few miles north of here, to Edinburgh. The postman said the fare to Pitlochry was fifty pence and he issued me with a smart purple ticket. The old lady beside me said that she found Calvine very quiet and out of the way. The only shop was half an hour's walk from her friend's house. She sighed with relief: 'That's my visit over for another year.'

At Blair Atholl another passenger got in: a frail, hypochondriac-sounding woman, very anxious to find a chemist's shop for some undisclosed reason. She had great difficulty sorting out the change for her ticket and, throughout the journey, complained of feeling sick and kept clutching at her throat, mumbling.

My neighbour had a good deal to say about the Commonwealth Games which were just about to begin in Edinburgh, and the number of tourists, and the Festival coming on soon after. 'Princes Street is a disgrace,' she confided. 'Do you know that some of the shops put out baskets of shoes on the pavement? That would never have been allowed before the War.'

In order to preserve some shred of hope for humanity, I must try to believe that there are worse things in life than shoe-baskets in the street.

The postman meanwhile regaled us with stories which illustrated the dangers of motorcycling. Many were his own adventures, such as the time he had been knocked down by a car which suddenly appeared from a side road. Had he been badly injured? 'Oh, no,' said the postman, shrugging the matter aside in the best stiff-upper-lip tradition, 'I just went straight over the bonnet.'

A pretty girl eating her lunch of bread and apples in a River Board van parked by the Moulin Road gave me some rather vague directions. She had heard of Kinnaird cottage, but she knew nothing of Stevenson's connection with these parts. Nor did a receptionist at Fisher's Hotel in Pitlochry, where Stevenson stayed for four days in June 1881 with his wife, Fanny, and 'Waggie', their Skye terrier. When I asked the receptionist if she could give me any information about RLS, she reached for the hotel register, began flicking through the pages and then asked blankly, 'Was he here not long ago?'

Her reply stands on a par with the answer a German friend of mine received when he asked a waitress in a big West Coast hotel whether he might have dinner earlier than usual, at about six-thirty. 'No,' said the waitress, 'we'll still be serving high tea.'

My friend had never heard the expression before and so he asked, 'What is the difference between high tea and dinner?'

The girl replied, 'About two pounds.'

The owner of a small guest house further down the road knew

Miss Robertson and her sister, Mrs Stewart, who lived at
Stevenson's cottage, and she told me exactly how and where to find
it. As it turned out, she also knew my parents.

The cottage looked very pretty. It was built on two floors with
overhanging eaves and a pitched slate roof with three small dormer-
windows in front. There was a rowan tree growing in one corner
and red and white roses trained up on either side of the bright red
front door. The garden was the good old-fashioned sort, with
marigolds and pansies and lobelias and alyssum in the flower beds
bordering the lawn. No one answered when I knocked and rang the
doorbell, so after a few tries I gave up and went and sat down at the
roadside. I sketched the cottage, then ate a roll filled with gammon
and sliced tomatoes for lunch. I found a bronze plaque screwed to
the garden wall bearing the following inscription:

> Robert Louis Stevenson lived in this house from the 7th of
> June to the 2nd of August 1881. 'We have a lovely spot
> here: a little green glen with a burn.... Behind, great purple
> moorlands, reaching to Ben Vrackie.... Sweet spot, sweet
> spot'. (Letter to Sidney Colvin.)

If I remember correctly, the plaque was put there to mark the fifty
years since Stevenson's visit. Miss Robertson later sent me a
privately printed pamphlet of seventeen pages written by Dr T.
Crouther Gordon about the time the plaque was made. Dr Crouther
Gordon described the cottage interior as it was in Stevenson's day:

> On the ground floor there was a drawing-room to the left
> and a dining-room to the right, and a small bedroom to the
> back of the house. Since then a porch has been added to the
> front door, a new bathroom put in, and an outhouse reared
> at the back.... There was of course no gas in the house and
> the visitors had to work with oil lamps, which to a mind like
> Stevenson's lent added gloom to his thinking. A fair stretch
> of garden runs from the front door to the High Drive, which
> leads over the moor to Kirkmichael. A handy little gate of
> wood allowed Louis to steal out of the side garden and up
> the glen.

According to Dr Crouther Gordon, the landlady's daughter at Kinnaird Cottage, Helen Sim, remembered that Louis and Fanny 'like to have big fires on both in their bedroom and sitting-room, with open windows'.

'The weather was fairly good in June, but July was damp and cold.' Stevenson caught a bad cold in his head and throat, which worsened his tuberculosis and which he never got rid of throughout his stay. At the beginning of August, he wrote to Colvin: 'I have had a brutal cold, not perhaps very wisely treated; lots of blood – for me I mean.'

Stevenson had left his sick-bed at Davos in May, according to Dr Crouther Gordon, 'with his hopes built up upon a highland holiday, suffused and radiated with sunshine'. Instead, at Kinnaird, he wrote to his friend Sir Edmund Gosse that he found himself 'being gently blown and hailed upon, and sitting nearer and nearer to the fire'. He was, as Dr Crouther Gordon reported:

> penned into a house not his own, by driving winds and dark, deluging clouds.... The younger Mrs Stevenson asked her mother-in-law when the Spring would begin.
> 'The Spring! Why, this is the Spring.'
> 'And the Summer, when will the Summer be here?'
> 'Well,' replied the more experienced lady, 'we must wait for St Swithin's Day. It all depends on what kind of weather we have then.'
> In due time the 15th of July arrived, and sure enough it poured ...

I finished my lunch, leaning over the field gate like a farmer, enjoying the view of the green Tummel valley and Pitlochry's grey rooftops.

On the way through Moulin, I noticed a polished brass plate on the door of a cottage next to the hotel; engraved on it in bold letters was THE ATLANTIC SALMON TRUST. I knocked but got no reply. The hotel manager suggested I try again. 'The secretary's car is over yonder, she can't be far away.' I walked back to the cottage and went upstairs to a landing which gave onto two rooms, one on either side, both empty. Just then the secretary came in and jumped with fright when she saw me looming above her. But when I explained my reason for being there, she gave me some booklets, including a study of *Salmon Stocks: A Genetic Perspective*, which explained the Trust's objective – 'to promote the conservation and enhancement of Atlantic salmon stocks … by fostering international agreements, EEC and domestic legislation and by stimulating scientific management and research'.

The Trust is a charitable organisation. I was amazed to find brochures advertising the Third International Atlantic Salmon Symposium to be held at Biarritz, the whole affair planned from this tiny cottage in a tiny village thirty-five miles from Perth. The secretary, Mrs Hinds, proudly showed me the brand-new office computer and said she was still finding her feet after nine years spent in Australia. The whole set-up was astonishing. I should like to have met the Trust's director, Rear-Admiral John Mackenzie, but he was 'out of town' at a meeting.

Today everybody was away.

1 August

Near the tumbledown Ruiclarchie bothy in Glen Bruar, I found a turf banking which faced the sun and sat sketching a flock of sheep grazing in the river meadows. The shorn ewes looked almost indecently naked compared to the lambs, which pranced about like balls of yellow cotton wool. Few sounds broke the afternoon stillness. The sheep's continuous melancholy bleating, the plash of the river, the flies and the blurred wind in my ear. Here was a glimpse of Arcady, the tranquil shepherd-life idealised by Greek myths. I daresay that was all very fine in the hot, dry mountains of the Eastern Mediterranean, but here in Scotland in the winter sleet and snow shepherding is a gruelling, unromantic business.

The straddle-legged patient ewes grazed while their lambs suckled, forcing their greedy muzzles hard against the mother's teat. A ewe would twist her body from time to time to discourage her hungry offspring.

I have often wondered why people dismiss sheep as stupid creatures. The sheep society, in fact, is highly organised. As with everything else in life, the great thing is taking time to sit quietly by and observe them. One of the shepherds remarked the other day: 'Sheep arna' fools. In their way, they are just as complicated as ourselves.' The shepherd is a good naturalist, very observant and knows what he is talking about.

2 August

On the other side of the hill, the river was in full spate after a night's heavy rain. The white spray crashing over the rocks in midstream exploded high into the air, showering the alders and stunted oaks along the river bank. The river writhed and roared like a prehistoric serpent in its death-throes, its greenish-brown coils slimy with foam.

At three, the sky darkened and a sudden blast of wind brought a terrific downpour which soaked me to the skin. I had been sketching the hills to the north from the shelter of an abandoned farm-trailer and what had begun as a crisp crayon-and-wash drawing was instantly blotted out in a mess of streaming colours. Such are the trials and tribulations of sketching in the open air!

Later on, when the sun broke through, I went down to the river and dried my clothes. Then I gathered bunches of leafy twigs and some wildflowers in order to make sketches of them. It was risky work, for the banks were steep and very slippery. Rain I don't mind a bit, although I must admit that one good drenching a day is plenty. A dousing when the river was in this fierce temper was quite another affair.

3 August

On the way to the Allt Sheicheachan burn this morning, one of the planks forming a wooden footbridge gave way, and my foot went through above the ankle. Had I lost my balance the result might have been awkward. As it was I got away with nothing more than a jarred knee and a bruised shin. My leg was a bit stiff for the next day or two, but this did not prevent me from getting about as usual.

At the bothy I met a young man who had driven up from Edinburgh for a day's hiking over Beinn Dearg. He had set himself a target: to climb Beinn Dearg and be home by dinner-time. 'My workmates can't understand why I come here,' he said. 'If I tell them I've walked so many miles or climbed so many hundred feet, they can grasp that. But as for the real reason I like doing it, that

means nothing.' When he spoke of the red hill, he pronounced Dearg like door, with a hard D. The Highlanders say it softly, like the J in jam.

The young hiker told me that he finds a weekend in the open essential after his five days' grind at the office. How he would feel after a week in London, which is twenty times the size of Edinburgh and a hundred times dirtier, I cannot imagine. Edinburgh is all swept and shining by comparison. The pace is slower and people in cars are apt to doze off at the traffic lights.

I tramped over the moor by a waterlogged, boggy path which began as a double track leading to the grouse-butts higher up. The broad track vanished after half a mile and the rest of the walk continued over grass and clumps of short, springy heather.

The piping cry of a bird sounded from the heather right at my feet. I stopped and looked down and then carefully scanned the moor all round, but saw nothing. A second call, a little fainter, came from fifty yards off behind a hummock and a second or two later I heard another, this time from much further away. There may have been more than one bird, after all, except that the cries seemed to fade in a way that suggested a bird in flight. It was possible that the sounds had been distorted by the wind or the surroundings, though I doubted it. Anyhow, the caller's identity remained a mystery.

A curious formation of large boulders above the river had been sculptured fantastically by centuries of weather. At first glance, they appeared to have been man-made. The flat crown of one of the rocks was dished and compartmented like an in-flight plastic lunch tray. Another was deeply etched with crosses very like the Union Jack. Yet another had been split horizontally like the gaping mouth of a whale. The place had an oddly disturbing atmosphere, like a graveyard by moonlight.

Coming back through the Whim Wood, a jay's rasping call pinpointed the bird as it landed on the outermost tip of a pine twig which flexed under its weight like a diving board, so much so that I half-expected the jay to turn a somersault and nose-dive into the burn below. Jays are very common in the woods just now.

A bright orange roedeer, the only female I've seen since arriving here, crashed away through the bracken, hurdling the wreckage of dead branches with ease.

4 August

The woods are green and lovely, with the trees in full leaf. The tangle of ferns and the long grass scattered with harebells makes an attractive picture and contrasts charmingly with the silvery salmon-pink pine trunks.

Where the woods end and the moors begin, I met one of the estate keepers and had a long discussion about the season's prospects. He told me that grouse-shooting is a washout this year. Instead the stalking will begin earlier than usual, about 14 or 15 August. There's no shortage of deer, anyhow.

The keeper is very interested in sporting pictures, although I suspect his motives are as much commercial as they are aesthetic. He runs across wildlife artists now and then in the course of his duties, and he keeps an eye open for any promising newcomer whose work is still fairly cheap but is likely to rise in value. Our conversation turned to a poor young man who for two years lived off turnips and potatoes and worked hard to make a success of his art. I heard recently that his paintings now fetch several thousand pounds apiece. The keeper said that he bitterly regretted not snapping up a few of the artist's early works when he had the chance. He was evidently determined not to make the same mistake twice, and asked a great many questions: whether I painted in oils, where I exhibited, and so on. I told him that he and I would certainly be old and grey before I made any money from art – if indeed I ever did – and he laughed.

The keeper was not to be put off so easily, however, and suggested that I might like to sketch one of his prize bullocks, 'a richt guid beast' with an unpronounceable Gaelic name which he had meant to show this year at Edinburgh, but for some reason or other didn't.

I wandered up over the moors beyond the Allt Féith nam Fearne burn and made a crayon drawing of a single hind feeding in a gully not far from the bridge where I had so nearly broken my ankle.

The hills were deserted and hauntingly beautiful. The moorland tramp was a summit of pleasure: the bright sunshine, the bees droning in the heather, the pipe of an oyster-catcher and the curlews' mournful wail.

I have worked out the sort of life that would suit me very well indeed. I'd spend the summers tramping in the Highlands when the weather is mild and the colours are richest. Come the autumn and winter, I'd migrate south to the Spanish sierras; either that, or some picturesque backwater of Provence. A mountain hut in the Pyrenees would make a fine retreat – somewhere near Héas perhaps, or the Val du Louron. These are a tramp's castles in the air: a bothy in the Perthshire hills, a Camargue *gardian*'s thatched *cabane*, or a shepherd's mountain *grange*. Of course, conveniences such as electricity and running water needn't matter in the slightest.

Looking through an album of newspaper cuttings, I found an article describing a splendid walk I made from Blair Atholl to Glen Feshie and the Pass of Gaick, exactly three years ago to the day. The article originally appeared in *The Scotsman* in a somewhat different form. Glen Feshie lies to the north of Glen Tilt and Glen Bruar, where much of this summer's tramping took place; while the Pass of Gaick lies roughly parallel with Glen Bruar, further to the west.

4 August 1983, at Blair Atholl
A swallow, framed by the pale quarter-moon, preened intently on a wire. The sunset wind hardly stirred the trees. The landscape lay motionless as a picture postcard. The swallow twittered, gaped and scratched its neck-feathers. I stood in the garden thinking about tomorrow's long walk through four glens as far as the Cairngorms and back.

5 August
A soft Atlantic wind blowing off the moor carried fresh breaths of grass and heather. A pair of red squirrels chattered angrily among the pine roots; orange-and-brown butterflies fluttered above the deer-fence and played hopscotch at my feet. Most wonderful! One of them settled confidingly on my shirt-sleeve. Frail whites, whose wings are no wider than a fingernail, blew about like tiny scraps of paper. Other butterflies, whose colour matched the harebells, danced feverishly among the verge-grass. I watched and took notes, wishing that I did not have to identify them afterwards. It seemed impolite, like forgetting the name of the person you're talking to....

A kestrel flew out from the banking just ahead, rose and soared in a great clockwise arc above the Banvie. Two small brown birds with scissor-sharp voices shot up from the heather at the same instant.

Their traces left an after-image in the sky, like entwined skeins of wool unravelling simultaneously.

Some distance beyond Bruar Lodge, the track I had been following reduced to a narrow path, a mere gash in the heather, strewn with pebbles. I skirted a nameless lochan with three islands, where mallard rode at anchor and moorhens scuttered in the reeds.... The path climbed a romantic gorge with a clear amber torrent splashing down between pink rocks and clumps of grey rowan sprayed with berries.... At the head of Glen Bruar where the path divided, I crossed the burn on stepping-stones and scrambled up 1,000 feet onto a bleak moorland. A few hundred yards of beaten track, a small cairn and some white stones set far apart signed the way to Glen Feshie.

The sun vanished behind a layer of heavy cloud which unrolled like sheets of tarpaulin from the west.... The peat ridges, maned with heather, were for all the world like the drills in a potato patch, but ten times magnified. Progress over these waves and troughs was laborious and slow. The low cloud hid every landmark for miles around and when it eventually lifted I found myself wandering off course. A snowfield I had been aiming for now reappeared much further to the west....

As the sky cleared, a shaft of sunlight focussed on three stags with bright tan coats which were feeding into the wind about half a mile away. The sunbeam dramatised the scene, giving an effect very like the Victorian engraving of a cathedral interior with light-rays slanting across the nave.

From the summit of Leathad an Taobhain, the Cairngorms spread before me, willow-patterned in white and blue and magnificently austere. A strong west wind whipped the north slopes sweeping down to Glen Feshie as I zig-zagged gingerly down through the deep, bushy bracken. The descent was mildly hazardous. My cleated boot-soles kept skidding and threatening to overturn on treacherous, half-buried stones; and the bulky rolled-up sleeping bag tied to my knapsack dragged me off balance each time I missed my footing.

A maze of boggy channels connecting with the River Feshie reflected the yellow evening light which turned the clouds of biting midges into a haze of golden rain. I had tramped for twelve hours

and had eaten nothing except for some cold baked beans washed down with a few cupfuls of water. There was no feeling of weariness yet, however. Only a pleasant sort of vacancy amidships, which proved the saying that the anticipation of a good meal is often better than the meal when it arrives.

I reached the shores of Loch an t-Seilich at 10 p.m. In the red sunset glow the hills opposite were photographed on its mirror surface. The wind had fallen and there was no sound of any kind, except the faint lapping of tiny wavelets on the shingle and the wingbeats of mallard which printed the still air.

Perhaps because I was now tired and hungry, or perhaps because the day had been almost too lovely to bear, I found myself suddenly aching for a friend's company. I drank in the scenery until my heart and mind were filled to bursting, and then I stood up and yelled, and the echoes rippled round the hills and sank away in the fading light like the threads of silver current in the darkening water. I yelled again and again for the sheer joy of it, and the echoes came back and made me feel the loneliness more than ever. Stephen Graham wrote how his friend, Vachel Lindsay, would sometimes yell like that among the high peaks of the Rockies; but his was a massive sound, like the roar of an avalanche or the crash of falling rocks. The poet spoke to the mountains in their own tongue.

That evening, if any sound broke the silence, it should have been a thunderous crowd-roar reverberating through the vast stadium of hills.

Gaick Lodge stood beside the loch shore where there was a wooden boathouse and an upturned dinghy beached nearby. At the lodge, the stalker offered me a night's shelter in the bothy. I ate my supper of corned beef and biscuits and drank the welcome pot of strong black tea which the stalker's wife very kindly provided.

Twice within an hour, shooting-stars flashed and disappeared.... And after that I stretched out in my sleeping bag, snug and well-fed, and slept soundly till daybreak.

5–6 August

The annual exhibition I share with several other painters has got off to a flying start at Beauly, near Inverness. John and Audrey Harrower, who have organised these shows for twenty-five years or more, asked me up for the night, and so I went.

Just as the train was leaving Blair Atholl, my father came running alongside and pushed an envelope through the open carriage window. It was a letter from Hamish Wallace, inviting me to tramp his beautiful deer-forest in Glen Urquhart. The postman had seen us driving to the station and had given chase, thinking the letter might be important.

Well, that's how they do things here in the country!

7 August

This morning, on my way through Glen Tilt towards Fealar, I passed some workmen repairing the damaged parapet of a fine eighteenth-century stone bridge at a bend in the river. As I approached, a white West Highland terrier puppy, tied to a fence-post, reared on his dumpy hind legs and started yapping. The puppy belonged to the foreman, who told me that its name was 'Cheeky'. 'Cheeky by name, and cheeky by nature,' said the foreman.

The week before, Cheeky had fallen into the Tilt when it was in spate. Incredible as it may seem, the little dog managed to swim across the current which swept him downstream for a considerable distance. His master found him afterwards, trotting up and down the opposite bank, safe and sound and none the worse for his adventure. It is amazing that Cheeky wasn't drowned at once. On the day in question, I had been sketching further along the glen, and the force of water was appalling.

A few miles north of the bridge, a little way from Forest Lodge, I noticed a hind lying by herself. There was something unnatural in the way she lay calmly staring at me. I wondered if she had been injured and walked slowly over to investigate.

The hind remained perfectly still and allowed me to come very close. Her flanks were scarred and mangy and she had a yellow plastic collar fastened round her neck. She was completely tame and let me stroke her head and pat her nose while she nuzzled the palm of my hand. The hind reminded me of another I found high up on the moors at Fealar, a year or two ago. The Fealar hind was unmarked and bore no traces of having been hand-reared. This incident was so unusual that it is worth describing in some detail.

On 16 May 1985, a little before midday, I forded the Tilt where it flows past the junction with Tarff Water near the famous waterfalls. Carrying my boots by the laces, I scrambled up the steep path flanking the gorge onto a broad moorland which stretched away to a mass of blue hills flecked with snow. It was a glorious day with rags of cotton cloud drifting lazily across the clear cerulean sky. When I wiped away the perspiration from my brow, my hands smelled of the sweet moorland grass and heather.

A herd of about fifty deer were spread out, feeding into the wind, across a wide bench of yellow turf. In the strong sunlight their coats looked ashy-pale. I remembered seeing the drawings of zebra and giraffe which the north-country naturalist, Abel Chapman, made in Kenya eighty years before; and how Chapman had shown the animals furthest away almost white, bleached of their strong markings by the heat-haze. In fact, many of the deer I was watching *were* pale-coated, but it interested me to see how the changes of light affected their colouring.

I sat down in the heather and re-tied my boots. The moor, which at first sight had appeared flat and featureless, actually consisted of numerous dips and rises intersected by tiny gurgling burns which glinted like broken glass between the tussocks. There were boulders of all shapes and sizes, covered with moss and grey and russet lichen. Patches of coarse straw-coloured grass divided the frizzy clumps of bell-heather. The path wound along the gorge for some distance.

I wandered along at a leisurely pace, taking in the fine wild scenery and thinking how fortunate I was to have the health and strength – and the time, moreover – at my disposal to go about this beautiful country as I pleased. Quite suddenly a solitary hind appeared, less than fifty yards ahead of me, grazing deep down in a hollow. The hind was well below the skyline and blended perfectly with her surroundings. At that instant, to my dismay, I felt the breeze against my neck as it came round to blow in the hind's direction.

Instead of dashing away as I expected, however, she continued to feed, moving gradually uphill from the hollow straight towards me. I stood perfectly still, watching her from the corner of my eye. The gap between us gradually narrowed. The hind advanced steadily. Forty yards; thirty; now barely twenty-five yards. Every now and again she lifted her head and gazed at me. The haughty, wide-eyed stare betrayed neither bewilderment nor fear. The hind strayed to right and left as she continued to approach me, feeding unconcernedly all the while. The effect was extraordinary. I do not possess a camera, but how I wished for one at that moment!

She fed along the ditch that bordered the path, where shoots of succulent grass grew among the water. At fifteen yards she paused again and carefully studied me. I could see that she was a perfectly normal, healthy animal. Her coat was a little ragged, which was common at this time of year, but otherwise she appeared to be in good condition. She changed her stance as she nibbled, sometimes bracing her forelegs stiffly apart, keeping her hind legs close together, sometimes turning back upon herself with one leg vertical and the others at angles.

Very slowly I eased my knapsack off my shoulders and undid the canvas straps without taking my eyes from the hind. In the excitement of the moment I dropped a pencil. Apart from flicking an ear, the hind paid no attention. I knelt and retrieved the pencil and then began to sketch her. She sauntered closer still – now ten yards, now five. I could see every detail of her ears and forehead. Her dark-brown eyes bloomed like the lenses of my binoculars; there was a dark Y-shaped marking between her eyes and nose. Her rubbery greyish-black muzzle, moist and grainy, twitched as she cropped the blades of delicious water-grass. I heard her molars

grinding, and glimpsed flashes of white teeth as she flexed her lips. She turned to left and right like a trained model, allowing me to sketch her in a variety of attitudes.

I found that she was composed of nearly as many straight lines as the more subtle curves and swellings. I thought how right the great wildlife artist Carl Rungius was when he stressed the importance of these straights. I drew as rapidly as possible, fearing that the moment could not last. In the end, the hind got so close to me that I had to step a pace or two backwards, simply in order to keep her in perspective. She fed abreast of me at two yards for several minutes. Then all of a sudden she wheeled sharply, clearing the ditch in a graceful bound, and trotted away, head erect, to the top of the rise. I followed and saw her cantering over the moor in the direction of the herd I had seen earlier in the afternoon.

My sketches show clearly what occurred, and yet in a sense I realise how worthless they are. The camera never lies, they say; however, my sketches could as easily have been made in a deer park, or a paddock like the one near Blair Castle. *Only they weren't,* and you must take my word for that.

8 August

The day started cloudy with a light drizzle blowing down the glen on a north-west wind.

In the woods I picked some wild raspberries for breakfast, which were tart and very good, and then I tramped along the river as far as Bruar Lodge. The sun broke through soon after midday, shining on the slender green stems of Parnassus grass, throwing a gossamer golden veil across the moor. I determined to make the most of the fine weather and so, after a bite to eat and a rest at the mountaineers' bothy, I set off in the direction of Bhagailteach hill and Pitagowan which lies on its far side.

Pitagowan is a tiny hamlet surrounded by trees, and from the hill top it looks like a clutch of eggs in a dark-green nest with the old military road to Inverness running by. This road is the earliest of its kind, built by General Wade in 1728. It divides the fields near Pitagowan like a broad farm-track which runs parallel to the modern A9 motorway.

At the crest of Bhagailteach I sat among the heather and gazed at the wonderful sunlit landscape of pastel-blue hills which marked the Pass of Gaick and Dalnamein. Ben Vrackie, Beinn Dearg and Schiehallion rose up sharp and clear in various shades of blue, ranging from pale sapphire to the deepest indigo. Their colours and shading changed continuously as the clouds massed and separated, forming and reforming in vast, drifting patterns – white, pearl-grey and primrose-yellow – across the scintillating blue ocean of sky.

The blue of the hills mixed with hazy sea-green and violet and the slowly moving shadows were filled with purple and reddish undertones, deepening and fading, brushed by the sunlit wind.

The scene was breathtakingly lovely. I felt at peace with the world, rejuvenated and perfectly content.

Two children – a thin, dark-haired girl of about eleven and a boy somewhat younger, tousled, freckled, with a shy gap-toothed grin – appeared out of the sun. They had light red and blue nylon haversacks strapped to their shoulders, and the girl struggled with a big Ordnance Survey map which, to her annoyance, kept blowing inside-out in the breeze.

I asked where they were heading for, and the girl replied that they planned to spend the night at a bothy – 'somewhere over there,' she said, gesturing vaguely with a bony finger. I knew that the mountaineers' bothy I had come from was locked. The only other one I could think of was at Allt Sheicheachan, a little to the east of Bruar, but the name meant nothing to them.

I asked: 'Are you out here all by yourselves?'

The boy piped up: 'Oh, no! The others aren't far behind us.' He added, grinning his gap-toothed grin, 'Sheila's carrying all our food. She'll be along in a minute.'

As he spoke, a big blonde teenager in a grey tracksuit hove in sight bent practically double under the weight of her huge pack, with four more children trailing at her heels. When she had got her breath back, Sheila explained that her father and mother had gone ahead to Allt Sheicheachan with the rest of the kit and that she and her brothers and sisters, with a couple of school chums, had arranged to meet up with them at tea-time.

'We've brought stacks of grub,' said Sheila, jerking a thumb at the groaning backpack. 'There's gammon steaks, baked beans, eggs and sausages. You name it – we've got it!' She was a cheery girl and very friendly, quite obviously in total command of the situation.

One of the youngsters, a pale-faced little boy with an old-fashioned pudding-basin haircut, had edged up close to Sheila while we were talking. He thrust a fragment of black stone towards me and mumbled something which I couldn't quite make out. Flakes of mica glittered in the sunshine as I turned the stone over in my hand.

'That's Stephen's treasure,' said Sheila. 'He found it on the way up.'

The child stared anxiously into my face, willing me to share his joy in the shining new object. Sheila said: 'Stephen's totally deaf, but he is learning to lip-read. If you speak to him very slowly, he'll understand.'

It was like being asked to speak into a microphone for the first time. Self-consciously, very deliberately, I said: 'Stephen, this stone is beautiful. Just look how the mica sparkles in the sun!'

He beamed at me. 'Yes, yes!' he burst out. '*Mica*!'

Meeting Stephen was one of the highlights of my summer's tramping. The child was so plainly delighted with everything he saw. Every experience, for him, was new and wonderful. And yet how much had been denied to him: the birds' singing, the sound of his friends' laughter, the trickling music of the burn. In the days that followed, I saw the landscape in a different light. I realised how much I had missed by taking things for granted. How, as a painter, I relied on touch and hearing besides visual impressions.

Stephen's world was as silent as the depths of the sea. Sound meant nothing to him, but perhaps the shapes and movements he saw and recognised in some way made up for this. I could listen to the river from a distance and picture in my mind the water flushing through stones or flowing smoothly down its pebbly bed. For me, the idea of 'river' meant instinctively combining the sight and sound of it. Perhaps Stephen *felt* sound in a way that I couldn't begin to comprehend. Perhaps the sunlight glinting on the stone fragment, for him, made a sort of music unlike anything I would ever know.

But what I do know for certain is that on that day Stephen was happy.

At Pitagowan I found a ruined cottage overgrown with nettles and rye-grass, with birch saplings poking up through holes in the roof. Marion, my mother's hairdresser, lives next door. She told me that the cottage used to be the local library. Marion is often very funny, most of all when she doesn't mean to be. When she told me about the library, she said: 'Och aye, it's true what I'm saying. A good many folk round about here used to read books.'

The television age has hit the country hardest, I think. The younger generation, like Marion, say: Why scrub our husbands' shirts when we can buy a washing machine on the never-never? Why walk when we can drive? Why bother with the small print when the world can be made to appear in banner headlines at the flick of a switch?

In one of the fields near Blair Castle, there were cars and shooting-brakes parked bumper-to-bumper and crowds of people dressed in bright colours milling everywhere. It was the final day of the World Archery Competition, and by chance I got talking to one of the contestants.

His name was Roger Cornfield, and he explained with no attempt at false modesty that he was among the top twenty professional bow-shots in America. When I showed more than a passing interest and asked a few questions, Roger warmed to his subject as only an American can, and proceeded to give me a crash-course in modern archery techniques.

Roger was 'in the military'. He wore a Johnny Appleseed peaked cap pulled down low over his eyes and a big square silver buckle on his belt like a Texas cowboy. He planned to retire from the army in a few years' time and devote himself entirely to archery. He told me that he owned a sports shop in Denver. 'The money's all in bow-hunting,' said Roger. 'I'll make a fair living. Won't be much, but that and my army pension will free me to concentrate on serious stuff.' By serious stuff he meant world-class tournament archery. Roger explained that there were about 250 professional archers in the United States, who shot an annual circuit of eighteen competitions.

Like the majority of target-shots, Roger used a modern 'Compact' bow with three strings, two of which operated a pulley. The pulley was roughly equivalent to the gears on a bicycle. Roger gave me a demonstration. The pulley ran on wheels fixed off-centre at the top and bottom of the bow-shaft. Its action reduced the strain of pulling his 56-pound bow by half. The strain was greatest, Roger explained, at the moment of releasing the arrow. Thanks to the pulley, the archer pulled only 28 pounds instead of the full 56, and as a result his aim was steadier and more relaxed. This device greatly improved the shooter's accuracy.

The drawstring which released the arrow had a little peep-sight attached to it with a plastic hood which acted as a sunshade. The optical sight was a work of art. It was set a fraction above the grip. A tiny pink bubble was centred in a magnifying lens with a spirit-level immediately under it. Once the windage-screws had been adjusted, the archer had only to heel his bow slightly into the wind to compensate for drift. Which, as Roger pointed out, meant very little unless the target was placed more than thirty metres away.

A short length of cord tied to a metal rod sticking out in front of the bow indicated which way the wind was blowing.

'All this seems a far cry from the days of Robin Hood and Roger Ascham,' I said, and Roger nodded.

'Mind you,' he went on, 'some archers still prefer the traditional English longbow. It's a fine instrument in the right hands, but compared to the Compact I use, it needs a lot of strength not just to pull it, but to hold it steady. Other folks like what we call the Curly bow, or the reverse-curve bow. That's the kind you may have seen in Japanese movies. The longbow has a wooden shaft. The Curly bow has a shaft of laminated wood. And the Compact bow is made of laminated strips of metal. That's about it, I guess.'

I told Roger that I remembered having read descriptions of flight shooting in Asia where the object was distance instead of accuracy. Roger said that the Asiatics had used a version of the Curly bow which they shot, lying flat on their back, with the bow-shaft braced against the soles of their feet. I said that the longest flight shot I had seen recorded by the ancients measured 876 paces. But Roger told me that nowadays the record stands at nearly a mile, and that 1,500-metre flight shots are quite common!

The arrows, Roger explained, were graded according to their diameter and wall thickness, as well as length and deflection. The arrow's deflection was measured by suspending a two-pound weight from the centre of the shaft, while the two ends were supported by a frame. 'Arrows are a subject all of their own,' said Roger. 'I could talk arrows and nothin' but arrows for hours together. There's so many different kinds. Everything from these lightweight alumin'um shafts I've been using today, right on up to the big wooden-shafted hunting arrow with a steel point, just like they used in medieval times.'

Roger was rather depressed about his performance in the World Competition. 'Today was better,' he grinned ruefully. 'Yeah, I guess I shot pretty good today. Earlier in the week it went just so-so. Trouble is, I've not had enough time for practice.'

Not without a hint of pride he told me that in general the best American shots tended to score ten to fifteen points higher in competition compared to the best British archers. On average, the Americans managed to score 550 out of the possible 560 points, which to me seemed incredible.

'Archery has always been a male-dominated sport,' said Roger, 'but some of the women are fine shots too.' There were two American ladies competing at Blair Atholl: Michèle Ragsdale, and Rose Jackson who won the Ladies' Championship.

I liked Roger Cornfield. But then, my heart goes out to enthusiasts everywhere. It doesn't matter what their particular interest might be, steam engines, rare books or botany. The enthusiast is always worth listening to. As a rule, the enthusiast is more spontaneous than his fellow men. When he gets going on his pet subject, he bares his soul. His heart is set afire.

I must say, I like American enthusiasts best. In Britain, we keep our guard up, like old-fashioned duellists, whereas the Americans drop their guard straightaway and tell it out.

9 August

A cool morning; the clouds high. Very warm as the day progressed.

I made yesterday's eighteen-mile walk in reverse: Struan and Pitagowan, up over Bhagailteach hill and along Glen Bruar. Yesterday I had the sun on my face. Today it shone down on my back and shoulders and the least effort soaked one's clothes in perspiration.

At Bruar Hotel I met Sheila and her small party of ramblers, all of whom waved and shouted and seemed pleased to see me again. The deaf boy, Stephen, came over at once and told me he'd lost his precious stone. 'Never mind,' I said, 'you'll find plenty more where that came from.'

Stephen shook his head. 'No, no,' he replied, frowning. 'We have to go home tomorrow.'

These simple sentences cost Stephen such effort, unlike Sheila's father, who sat drinking cold beer at a white-painted garden table, a big fat loose-jowled man wearing spectacles, who took no part in the conversation. How he had managed the walk from Bruar to Allt Sheicheachan and back I cannot imagine. The effort of raising his beer glass appeared almost too much for him.

There were patches of green and yellow light dappling the hills to the west of Schiehallion, very like the wave-lights reflected on a boat at its moorings.

In the evening, to pass the time, I totted up the various mileages over the previous weeks. The first week made 60 miles; the second week 79; 71 the third week, and 95 the fourth. The fifth week added 104. To date, I found I had tramped over 400 miles. The longest day covered 27 miles and the daily average has worked out at about 11.

10 August

Every morning I have begun the day with a few simple exercises: running on the spot, touch-your-toes, turning from side to side with the arms at full stretch like a propeller. My father is a great believer in deep breathing, so I followed his example. It was extraordinary how the joints still creaked after a night's sleep, after so much loosening up and hard walking up hill and down dale! So much for the 400 miles....

Today in Glen Tilt, as I was approaching Forest Lodge, a big maroon Citröen swept out of the yard and disappeared through the trees in a cloud of dust. A mile or so further on, I saw the car parked off the track near the river, where there were two men fishing knee-deep in the water.

I was about to make a short detour across a bend in the track so as not to disturb them when one of the fishermen clambered onto the bank and waved and called me over. He was short and bulky with crinkly grey hair; I guessed in his late fifties. He and his companion came from Toulon. He told me that they leased Forest Lodge every year for a week's salmon fishing, always at the same time just before the shooting season got under way. Their wives did not like fishing and stayed at home.

'We have already catched one solomon,' he announced. 'There are also many trouts in the river, but we like the solomon better. Solomon is the *roi des pêches*!' He looked astonished when I said that I had only ever fished for trout. Solomons never. It was as though I'd said that I liked shooting poultry instead of pheasants.

When I added that I was very far from being an experienced fisherman, however, the Frenchman nodded. 'I quite understand,' he said, patting my shoulder and grinning. 'The solomons are difficult, even for Jean-Pierre and myself who know them.' Each time he began a sentence, his eyes popped, as though someone had goosed him. He always seemed on the point of confiding some secret of tremendous importance. I asked him whether he and his friend, Jean-Pierre, had tried deer-stalking, which is particularly good on the Atholl ground. But he shook his head vigorously and replied, 'No, monsieur. We do not care for the *haunting*. Solomon is quite enough.'

At Tarff, I copied out an inscription on a bronze plate fixed to the suspension bridge below the Falls. It ran as follows.

> This bridge was erected in 1886
> With funds contributed by
> His friends and others and by
> The Scottish Rights of Way Society Ltd
> To commemorate the death of
> FRANCIS JOHN BEDFORD, aged 18,
> Who was drowned near here
> On 25th August, 1879.

Two more fishermen, who had been resting on some stones near the bridge, got up and moved away as I appeared over the rise. In the lead was a tall, heavily built man in well-cut tweeds with a brown window-pane check and shiny brown boots. The other man carried their rods folded away in green canvas cases fastened with linen ties. The big man had a pair of binoculars, which looked like wartime naval-pattern 7 × 50s, slung across his chest; and he used a long shepherd's crook tipped with a ram's horn to steady himself on the narrow path leading down to the river. The two forded the Tilt, boots and all. They were very sure footed. English upper-middle-class was stamped all over them. They never so much as nodded, let alone pass the time of day, and I thought, what a contrast to the jolly pair from Toulon....

I took off my boots and socks and paddled in the ice-cold water, which was a rich tawny colour here, streaked with pale amber, rippling topaz and amethyst, dappled with the white and blue reflections of the sky. A sparrow hawk swooped down low over the water and landed on a dead branch where it sat for a few moments, ruffling its feathers, turning its head this way and that, before it glided away again down-stream.

Coming back by Forest Lodge later in the day, I found the two Frenchmen smartly dressed in St Hubert green jerseys with military-style green canvas shoulder patches, green worsted breeches and stockings to the knee. They were busy taking photographs of each other in the courtyard. They ran round and round, laughing and striking all sorts of ridiculous poses – mostly the 'alone-I-did-it' variety – brandishing their rods and, to my surprise, a shotgun. Goodness knows if their friends in Toulon got the impression that in Scotland we shoot salmon as well as hooking them. An eight-pounder they'd landed might have been bagged on the wing!

When my father-in-law was in Labrador before the War, carrying medical supplies to the outlying settlements, he often tramped all the daylight hours in snow-shoes with his sixteen-year-old guide, Timoshé. He confessed that he sometimes shot salmon where they came leaping in mid-air at a waterfall. There was no sport in this, but after the day's long slog in deep snow, they were so exhausted and hungry that getting a meal was all that mattered. Bears catch flying salmon in their paw. Using a charge of number six shot was not so very different.

The meadow-pipits flicked in tiny spurts from boulder to boulder ahead of me all the way down. Zig-zag, spurt, zig-zag, spurt; tiny bursts of wild chirruping where they landed. It was a game of follow-my-leader which we all enjoyed.

Below Marble Lodge, a family came trudging by – father in shorts, mother enormously fat and sweating, and their twelve-year-old son, who was tired and bored and getting to the bad-tempered stage. Father began exploring a midge-ridden, boggy meadow for a campsite. Mother said that they had come up by train that morning from Dundee and had walked the six miles up the glen from Blair Atholl. She and Father were weighed down with the inevitable backpacks, stuffed with tins and packets of digestive biscuits. These packs must have tipped the scales at fifty pounds apiece, probably more.

Mother enquired how far I had walked that day and I told her nearly thirty miles. Four hundred in thirty-two days, I added boastfully. She misunderstood and gasped. 'Fower hunder' miles in twa days!' she exclaimed. 'My, that's an awfy lot!' I agreed, it was *rather* a lot. So reputations are made and lost!

One of the best day's tramping I have made in recent years led through Glen Tilt and up over the Fealar moors towards Carn an Righ.

I had been much interested by W. McCrombie Smith's book, *The Romance of Poaching in the Highlands*, published in 1904; especially a chapter entitled, 'Lonavey, or a Poacher of the Olden Time'. McCrombie Smith described Lonavey's hideout, a cave in the Atholl hills where the sun shone through its narrow opening on only one day of the year. Lonavey always placed his treasured matchlock gun so that the sun would shine upon it on the longest day, if the weather was clear. For centuries the location of this cave remained a mystery, but according to McCrombie Smith, in 1904, there were two men in Blair Atholl who knew of the cave's existence and, moreover, how to find it.

In the late spring of 1985, about the time I had my adventure with the Fealar hind, I resolved to explore Lonavey's country and at the same time find out more about his strange life, and I wrote and illustrated a long article about it at the time.

When I was a boy, I remember someone telling me that a man's capacity for good invariably equalled his capacity for wickedness. If my informant ever read *The Water Babies*, he must have agreed with Kingsley that 'a keeper is only a poacher turned outside in, and a poacher a keeper turned inside out'.

The annals of poaching in the Highlands, as we might expect, have been cloaked in mystery. A handful of names, people, places and events stand out sharply like the great hills which dominate the wilderness of moor. How these free-foresters of days gone by lived is hard to discover, for in the world of poaching, legends are far commoner than facts.

In the early part of the seventeenth century, a notorious free-forester named Ian Mackeracher and his burly cousin, Mackeracher Ruadh, ravaged the Atholl hills for many years in pursuit of deer. Ian Mackeracher's nickname 'Lonavey' derived from the Gaelic *lonach fiadh*, which literally translated means 'greedy for deer'. The name had been earned by his prowess as a stalker and his obsession for the chase.

As far as I know, the exact dates of Lonavey's birth and death are unrecorded. He lived through the reigns of Queen Elizabeth and King James, and died while Charles I was still on the throne. Apart from his more outrageous exploits, Lonavey remained a shadowy, mythogenic figure, a rascal I found both attractive and intriguing.

During my tramps across the Atholl ground, where much of Lonavey's time was spent, I often tried to visualise him, and recreate something like flesh and blood from his vaporous biography.

In his youth, while he was still inexperienced and reckless, Lonavey was caught after a raid and his left hand was amputated at the wrist as a punishment. It seems likely that the cruel sentence embittered him. He rejoined his cousin and together they intensified their poaching, often taking tremendous risks, even to hunting down the largest and most renowned stag in Atholl, a monster which fatally gored Mackeracher Ruadh during its death-throes.

For the remainder of his career, Lonavey lived and stalked alone. He either slept in the heather or foraged from his secret headquarters, a rank-smelling cave hidden in the far depths of the hills.

Over the years, Lonavey became as wild as the animals he hunted. It was not very difficult to picture him: small and weatherbeaten, barefoot, ragged and dirty, the withered stump of his left arm gloved in a strip of deerskin. Strands of dark, matted hair fell to his shoulders, and his bright eyes, forever ranging the horizon, were probably dark blue, as piercing as those of any Highlander today. By then he had likely forgotten the ways of ordinary conversation.

Lonavey possessed two formidable weapons: a heavy matchlock with a long barrel (this at a period when firearms were still a novelty and scarce), and a murderous dirk, sixteen inches long, made from the blade of a sword. The stalking art may have been inherited from his father. The gun too, perhaps.

Lonavey lived the life of a troll. I imagine him as a pagan and a hill-pantheist; a shy recluse whose insatiable bloodlust brought momentary satisfaction, but yet denied him peace of mind. Hunting the deer and a passion for freedom were the mainspring of Lonavey's wild life. In some respects he had been a menace. Yet at least one of the Earls of Atholl admired his talent for marksmanship enough to persuade him to enter an annual shooting contest when Atholl employees challenged the crackshot English harvesters who came north each year to mow and cure the haycrop. Until then, the English journeymen had swept the board.

When the Englishmen saw Lonavey's quaint technique, they laughed at first. The one-armed poacher stepped back twenty paces from the firing-line, then moved rapidly, crouching, cautiously peering ahead of him, exactly as though he were manoeuvring towards a stag. He pounced forward in a series of lightning-fast movements, deftly planted the forked stick gun-rest and lit the powder charge. (On the hill, the deer, shocked by a man's sudden appearance at such close range, usually froze for several seconds before bounding away and in that brief instant the stalker had his chance.)

A flash, a loud bang, a pall of smoke. Up went a great shout! Lovaney's bullet had scored a perfect bullseye. The English haymakers were defeated, and the grateful Earl of Atholl promised in future to ignore Lonavey's activities, provided that he undertook not to poach the deer excessively, as before.

The pact was honoured on both sides. But some years afterwards, the Earl's ruthless successor had Lonavey arrested and sent in chains to Perth prison, where the little man died, like a caged wild bird, his heart and spirit broken.

Sensing that his capture was imminent, Lonavey hid his beloved matchlock and dirk in the secret cave for future use, having first preserved them carefully with a coating of deer-fat. Later, when he realised that he would never be set free, he confided the cave's position to a cell-mate who, after his release, told others but left the cave and Lonavey's possessions undisturbed.

Two hundred and fifty years after Lonavey's death, about 1875, a Mackeracher kinsman, the notorious poacher and Scottish champion rifleman, John Farquharson, accidentally stumbled on the legendary hideout while himself being closely pursued by three of the Atholl keepers after killing a stag in the hills of north Glen Tilt.

Farquharson had dropped out of sight behind a boulder, on the south-east shoulder of Carn an Righ. Glancing frantically about him, he noticed an opening, rather like a fox's earth, beneath an overhanging ledge. He wriggled inside downwards, headfirst, and found himself at the base of a rock-chimney, high enough to stand up in.

Farquharson still felt vulnerable. If his followers should happen to glance down, they would surely see his legs and feet. In desperation he clawed the rock above him for a hand-hold in an effort to haul himself clear of the entrance hole. He found a deep cavity which turned out to be the throat of a passage leading to a large cavern.

As soon as the baffled keepers had departed, Farquharson struck matches and step by step explored the gloomy interior of the cave. The chamber measured fourteen feet by twelve, with a roof which sloped from eight feet down to five. A narrow fissure in the rock admitted the merest trace of daylight. On one side, Farquharson saw a natural bench of rock like a day-bed, on which lay the rusted, wormed remains of a long-bladed dirk and gun. John Farquharson knew then that he had discovered Lonavey's cave and the old free-forester's precious relics.

For a time, the discovery enhanced Farquharson's already widespread reputation. He exhibited his trophies and took a great delight in misleading anyone who tried to make him disclose the cave's whereabouts. He described the details of its interior which McCrombie Smith recorded in his *Romance of Poaching in the Highlands*; but the precise location Farquharson kept secret, for, after all, the cave had become as useful to him as it had been to Lonavey centuries before.

The puzzle fascinated me. I searched a score of likely places in vain. But I consoled myself with the thought that, had I found the cave too easily, its discovery would have been robbed of much of its significance and excitement.

Eventually, in 1985, I made up my mind to try again. I combed libraries and museums in London and Edinburgh for information, and I questioned everybody I could think of between Perth and Inverness who might provide me with some fresh clues. After a time, I found a man whose knowledge of the Atholl hills and their remote corries was greater than that of any man living and who suggested the most hopeful area in which I might begin the search.

I packed a sleeping bag and sketchbooks and enough food for three days; and after ten hours' hard tramping I reached a beautiful, high wild country cut by streams and gorges. In places the going was by far the roughest I had ever attempted. The heather sprang from waves of sodden peat, some of them a yard deep. I sank above my calves in the open, marshy ground and every few miles faced steep scrambles across slide-rock lying at angles of more than forty-

five degrees, which gave under me at every step and where a fall would almost certainly have meant serious injury.

The place I was looking for lay several hundred feet above the moor, on the south face of a hill shaped like an upturned boat. It seemed unlikely that the site would have been much higher up, since Farquharson would only have killed stags within reach of his pony, tied or hobbled in a gully, waiting to carry off the carcass before it was discovered.

As soon as I reached the hill, I realised that I was very little further forward. Like the proverbial needle in a haystack, the cave entrance lay buried beneath an avalanche of shale. It was a terrible, stark region. There were no birds; no sound of any kind except the wind. I looked up and saw a line of seven large snowfields. The third from the right resembled in outline a cave-painting of running bison.

The clouds dispersed towards evening and the sunset was magnificent. I remembered that it was Ascension Day. In my notebook I wrote: 'Spires and battlements of bluish-grey, and the sky all brilliant peach-pink and gold. Sun-streamers like spotlights bleaching the landscape and the hills like translucent strips of coloured cellophane, receding and fading in the distance ...'

After the sun had set, the wind got up and it grew chilly. I camped out under a blanket of thick cloud and wondered how long it would stay dry. However, there was no rain that night, but when I woke at dawn the sleeping bag was drenched with dew. I brewed some tea and munched a few slices of corned beef. By sunrise I was back among the slide-rock, searching in the hard grey light for the cave's tunnel-mouth under its jutting slab beside the great rock where Farquharson had hidden. If Lonavey's hideout existed at all, it was here, a few hundred yards to right or left, somewhere on the hillface above or below me.

The hours dragged past and I began to realise that, without some definite reference point, it would be sheer chance if I hit upon the cave.

Two stags in velvet appeared and stood brazenly observing me at 400 yards. I sketched them, all the while imagining that I saw Lonavey's stooping, predatory form aligning his long gun-barrel from the cover of a rock.

The stags cantered off downhill, and I went on searching; but I did not find the cave. Providence has been kinder since and I have been told of a man, who by rights should be ancient, white-haired and feeble, a quiet-spoken man who before he dies might one day reveal the secret. Thanks to him, I am nearer than ever to discovering Lonavey's cave. And yet, foolish and romantic as it sounds, I almost hope that we never meet and that the secret cave remains a mystery.

Lonavey's relics, too, have disappeared. McCrombie Smith wrote: 'the rust-eaten remains of the gun and dirk were often looked at, and considerable care taken of them, but the novelty of seeing them by the few who were accorded the privilege wore off, and especially when it was seen that with the exception of the thick end of the barrel, all the other parts of the gun and dirk were far too decayed to bear any attempt at cleaning and preserving, they were relegated to out-of-the-way corners amongst other disused odds and ends of iron, until the lock and forepart of the barrel and the entire dirk crumbled into mere scales of rust. The last time the breech end of the barrel was observed by its discoverer it was being used as a poker! He took it and put it aside, but one day a sister, engaged in spring-cleaning, came upon it and heedlessly threw it into a small tarn near the house. When Farquharson learned what had become of it, the inexcusable carelessness that did not preserve, as long as possible, some part of so interesting relics, was bitterly regretted. The cave, however, still remains, and the foregoing traditions prove that, in one part of Athole [sic] at least, the name and fame still survive of Ian Mackeracher, the famous Lonavey.'

11 August

Today I took things easy after the last couple of days' tramping which together knocked up forty-five miles.

What had threatened to become a blister at the joint of my big toe and the sole of my right foot came to nothing. A little discomfort, but no more than that. I felt rather smug, having covered the distance from London to Glasgow and more, that I had so far escaped blisters and corns and other aches and pains, which did not seem too bad after six months in the city.

In the morning I worked up a sketch of nineteen stags I had made in Glen Bruar on 3 August. I altered the groupings somewhat for the sake of the composition, and kept the tones fairly muted with dullish browns and blues and plenty of mist and low cloud in the background. For some reason, bright strong colours seldom do for painting deer.

Later in the day I found a man and his two teenage sons playing football on the lawn in front of the castle. Perhaps I am missing something obvious, or else I'm just plain bigoted, but for the life of me I cannot see why people should come so far to visit a fine, historic building, full of interesting things, and then play football. The castle grounds were little more to them than a pleasure park with a grander sort of background....

12 August

The Glorious Twelfth!

I rose at first light as usual and did exercises. I had paid the penalty for yesterday's slackness, and this morning I really knew that I had feet and ankles and knee-joints, all of which needed waking up and all of which responded to the dawn Reveille with bad grace!

From Pitlochry, I walked up the Moulin road towards Ben Vrackie. The road branched away through the trees and continued up a steep, stony, forking path, where the tree roots and slabs of stone formed steps and leafy branches of beech and oak swept down low with luminous green shadows falling between the patches of strong sunlight. The woods were carpeted with ferns and brambles and to the right of the path a tiny burn trickled by, adding a simple, lyrical enchantment to the surroundings.

I lunched sitting on a stile where the rolling purple moors began. Then I climbed the stile and struck away across the rising folds of heather to the mountain whose summit cairn sparkled in the sun like a beacon.

To my surprise, a summer-seat had been set down at the crest of the moor, carefully positioned so as to give a splendid view of the Tummel Valley and the hills beyond. The seat bore an inscription: IN MEMORY OF TERENCE TOOLE, RAAF, 1947–72. Whoever he was, Terence Toole certainly had an eye for country, and many a hillwalker since must have had cause to be grateful for the thoughtfulness of his parents who had put the seat there.

Over another stile by a field-gate and on uphill by way of a path to the rim of a wonderful moorland glen on the south side of Ben Vrackie. There were two small bright-blue lochs, the furthest away with a red-roofed summer house beside it. The summer house was a simple structure with no walls and the roof was supported by wooden pillars. Ben Vrackie towered above, its flanks streaming down in grey scree with the usual accompaniment of sun-bleached turf and heather, and a path scored in its side which divided halfway in a maze of side-tracks like the roots of an immense fossilised tree.

Instead of climbing Ben Vrackie, on this occasion I contented myself by sketching it and the views of the glen. Numbers of children and grown-ups passed to and from the base of the hill while I sat on a boulder soaking up the marvellous scenery. One of them, a flaxen-haired woman of about thirty-five, strode up and we exchanged greetings and chatted briefly. The woman was Prussian: a classic fraulein, with steely-blue eyes and firm, well-chiselled features. She was tanned and lean and wore a blue cotton tee-shirt and thick blue corduroys. She looked quite capable of commanding a Panzer division.

'Ach so,' she replied to my question, in perfect stereotype. 'The path to the top is really quite tough, you know.' From where I was sitting, it appeared to be almost vertical. 'I stayed only one hour at the summit,' she said, 'but alas, it was all the time misty.' She meant 'hazy', for the weather could hardly have been more perfect. I thought to myself, if she says the path is tough, she means *tough*.

The way up Ben Vrackie is actually quite straightforward, albeit a fairly stiff climb. There are three stages. The first stage is by the frayed paths which look like exposed tree roots; then round a shoulder of the hill; and after that by a zig-zag route to the top. The way down is easier, but is hard on the back of one's knees. Ben Vrackie is not particularly high – about 2,500 feet – but, as the locals say, 'enough to be going on with'.

On the way back, I slipped and fell flat on my back in a muddy puddle, where the outfall from a burn had spread across the path. I felt relieved that the flaxen-haired fraulein wasn't there to see it.

I sketched the jagged outline of Creag Bhreac from below Meall na h-Aodainn Móire and afterwards managed a better crayon sketch of Ben Vrackie from the Moulin road, where it turns off to the Pitlochry Hydro Hotel. The sky colour nearly matched the colour of the hills. When Robert Louis Stevenson spoke of the purple heather moors in July 1881, he must have found the heather coming into bloom much earlier than it did this year. Coming down from Ben Vrackie, I heard a flutter of gunshots in the distance. There had been nothing very glorious about the Twelfth this year – except for the weather – and I hoped the sportsmen, whoever they were, felt adequately compensated.

13 August

Today I walked as far as Edradour, which I believe I am right in saying is the smallest distillery in Scotland. Edradour's financial director, Gordon Ross, and his assistant, Mrs Barbara Sadler, gave me some interesting information about the place.

Originally, the small farmers living all round Edradour contributed to the barley yield which served the distillery, generally in order to reduce their debts. In 1825 they formed a company which took the business in hand.

Edradour has never been a major distillery. Its annual output is approximately 78,000 litres – which to me sounded enormous until

I was told that the next largest distillery in size after Edradour produces half a million litres a year. Although the distillery is named after the burn which flows past the still-house and the other buildings standing in a hollow at the foot of the Moulin road, the water used for making Edradour's famous malt whisky comes from a spring which rises far out on the moors.

There is a workforce of three. Most of Edradour's output is exported to the USA and the rest is sold in prestigious London stores such as Harrods and Fortnum and Mason.

Talking of statistics, the parent company, Aberlour Glenlivet, itself produces three million barrels annually. These are the Rolls Royce and Bentley of Scottish malt whiskies. The distillery is well worth a visit and, for anyone who enjoys whisky, I am told that a taste of Edradour's ten-year-old malt, which is sold at Heather Bank Cottage nearby, is an unforgettable experience.

14 August

I slept soundly and got up at ten minutes to seven as usual and did my routine exercises and deep breathing. It rained a little during the night, but by 11 a.m. it was fine and sunny. Going through Glen Banvie by the high track, a greyish-brown lizard scuttled across a few feet in front of me and disappeared into the grass. I hunted the lizard for a while, but failed to find it.

A herd of thirty-five stags feeding downhill to the burn let me approach to within 500 yards before they cantered away, back the way they had come, and vanished over the rise. The stags grouped and regrouped as they went, leaving one or two beasts in the rear which eventually joined the rest. At about a thousand yards the stags pulled up and turned to look at me. One or two began feeding, but the majority remained on the alert. I remembered that the stalking season had begun and so perhaps this herd had been shot at already. They were on the *qui vive*, anyhow.

One of the stags, a big heavy-bodied animal, had a very distinctive dark red coat. The others were mostly orange-russet. Their white rumps and pale inside legs stood out very conspicuously in the strong sunlight. A few stags had nicely shaped antlers, but they

were too far away for me to be able to count the points through my 6 x 30 binoculars. My eyesight seems to be deteriorating year by year, and I think this comes from writing and reading in bad light in a succession of dark houses. It is a nuisance having to carry a spectacle case, but there it is. *Anno domini* catches up with us all and, as somebody said the other day, it usually travels in company!

Moving away at speed, the herd flowed up and over the crest of the hill in perfect unison. Flowed is the only possible description. The stags seemed to drift away like red smoke. Only when I tried to concentrate on a single beast did the powerful lunging stride over the heather and rock become apparent. At a canter, the deer carry their heads erect, enough to delight any deportment mistress at a finishing school. Going hard over the rougher ground, the stags pitched and rose like the waves of the sea.

I saw more deer further to the west on the high slopes of the Banvie moor. Whether or not this herd had been part of the original group of thirty-five, I cannot tell. When I say 'the high slopes' I am speaking in relative terms. As a matter of fact I was surprised to find the deer so low down, for as a rule they keep to the high tops in summer, where the breeze rids them of insects.

The sunlight made the stones very white, especially in the distance. So when I made a watercolour sketch of the stags later on, I took a leaf from Johnny Millais's book and laid on Chinese white for all I was worth.

Later in the afternoon, as I was returning along the Banvie track, I saw the herd of thirty-five again, a hedge of antlers above the skyline, then their bodies coming slowly into view. They were no more than 250 yards away this time and when they spotted me they fled immediately, racing down at full gallop over the track and the low grassy flats to the burn, where they wheeled sharp right and jumped the water. The stags continued at full speed straight up the hillside opposite, where a flock of five sheep, startled by the sudden invasion, galloped towards them instead of taking to their heels the other way, and ran parallel with the stags as far as the ridge.

Last night's rain had softened the earth on the track, liquefying the dust to marbled streams which carried imprints of the stags' long pointed hooves. The deeper, splayed-toe impressions showed where they had struck the track in flight.

This evening I supped on wild raspberries and took some home, wrapped in my plastic specimen-bag, which my mother made into a delicious pudding with vanilla ice-cream and meringues.

15 August

I only tramped a few miles today and instead spent the morning trying to sketch the stag herd. My first effort was poor; muddy and lifeless. After a second shot and then a third, I managed a sketch in less than half an hour, which got somewhere nearer the mark. It's always the same story: the considered, cold-blooded efforts stiffen up and the movement freezes; they lose the action and vitality of the quick sketches almost entirely. I noticed swallows flying and diving all round the house and the farmstead at the end of the road. They perched twittering on the electricity wires. Their song is instantly recognisable. The swallows look just like miniature, sapphire-blue parakeets. They are my favourite of all the birds.

16 August

It poured with rain all night. The fields in front of our house were half-flooded. At seven, I saw a small flock of geese flying over from the south-east. Everything was drenched and dripping. Along the fencing-wires at the edge of the field, beads of water sparkled in the watery sun. The grass was all wet and shining as though it had been polished. Midges were dancing in peppery clouds above the puddles in the drive.

The Grouse Ball, a great social occasion, was held last night at the castle. The house was floodlit and there was a big white marquee set up on the croquet lawn. Several hundred guests paid £40 a head for a buffet supper, dancing and a champagne breakfast. The proceeds go to charity. Grouse-wise the whole thing was rather a non-event, for the season locally has been a disaster.

By contrast, Raoul Millais wrote telling me that Invermark had had a record year. The next-door estate, on the other hand, fared little better than the Atholl moors. Raoul is now in his eighties and

is the most delightful, generous-hearted person imaginable. He is a fine painter and has turned out some marvellous canvasses of deer and racehorses in his day. His father was the great John Guille Millais, who wrote some of the best sporting and travel books ever produced. Much of their unique charm lies in the wonderfully observed drawings and paintings with which Millais illustrated his writing. His South African shooting book, *A Breath from the Veldt*, first published in 1895 in folio, not only has one of the best titles I have ever heard of, but also describes in fascinating detail a year's trekking and hunting in the wilderness during an era which has sadly vanished forever.

Raoul, like his father (who, I should add, died in 1931, ten years before I was born) has a keen sense of humour. A year or two ago he wrote saying that he'd had a hard week's shooting in the Highlands and that he had spent every night in a different house, ending up somewhere in Caithness. He added a postscript: 'I expect we shall have the memorial service at Wick!'

A big load of sawn logs arrived from Dunkeld in the afternoon – about two and a half tons, which the lorryman dumped near the woodshed. Mum and Dad and I worked hard getting the dry wood into the shed and stacking it along the walls. We managed very well, chain-gang fashion, and cleared the best part of a ton before the rain started. Dad organised the shed while Mum and I gathered the flat chips and separated these from the rounder heavy logs, clearing the pile from back to front, and getting a few nasty slivers – 'skelfs' as they are known here – in our fingers. A 'skelf' jammed under a fingernail is about the vilest thing I can imagine.

The evening turned out fine and mild, with a strong scent of wet pine and the tangy odour of woodsmoke in the air.

Speaking of the Grouse Ball reminds me that in the castle library there are something like sixteen copies of William Scrope's classic, *The Art of Deerstalking*, which first appeared in 1838. Many of them are signed and annotated by Scrope himself.

I began my tramping days in the glens round Blair Atholl about the time I rented Marble Lodge in Glen Tilt, which Scrope dismisses in his book as 'a mere station'. The ground I have been describing, where much of last year's summer tramping was done, is the same ground over which Scrope stalked and fished for ten glorious seasons, beginning in 1822 when he was already fifty years old.

In a sense, I suppose that Scrope and Lonavey Mackeracher were merely two sides of the same coin. Scrope paid handsomely for his sport, while Lonavey claimed it as his right. Both men were excellent stalkers and fine shots. Both were eccentrics in their way. But, above all else, the lure of the high hills and the deer became their overwhelming passion.

It is probably true that William Scrope was the father of deerstalking as we know the sport today. His story is an interesting one and well worth telling again.

About two hundred years ago, the red deer population in the Highlands had sunk to its lowest ebb after the hills began to be cleared wholesale for sheep. Yet by the turn of the century, the revolutionary concept of letting privately owned deer forests – and their consequent improvement – had effected a marked recovery. The Highlands attracted an ever-growing number of wealthy English sportsmen willing to pay substantial rents, and the new source of revenue helped to create seasonal as well as permanent employment for the hitherto starving crofters, who acted as ghillies, ponymen and foresters. The crofters disliked the distant, haughty manner of these visitors, but accepted them as a necessary evil. They despised many of their employers, who rose late, plunged clumsily about the heather, missed easy shots and whiled away the lengthening autumn darkness with diversions such as cards and whisky.

Nevertheless, on the tenants' behalf the landowners cut tracks across the moors, built lodges, determined their hitherto vague boundaries and keepered their ground. After only a few decades, the free-roaming wilderness of the eighteenth century had all but completely disappeared. Enterprise, like a sharp-toothed comb, had smoothed and ordered the tangled desolation of moor and mountain.

In the management of estates, as in the quality of visiting sportsmen, there had of course been notable exceptions. Great deer forests such as Atholl, Black Mount and Mar had been carefully preserved for deer throughout many generations. It was to the Duke of Atholl's factor that William Scrope (pronounced 'Scroop'), an English landowner, artist and classical scholar, wrote in the spring of 1822 enquiring after sporting rights on any vacant and preferably extensive ground within the 100,000-acre estate.

Scrope's friend, Sir Walter Scott, added an enthusiastic letter of recommendation. Thus the late summer of that same year found Scrope, one morning before daybreak, wending his way by pony from Blair Castle, through Glen Banvie, towards Bruar Lodge which for the next ten seasons would become his picturesque and remote headquarters. In *The Art of Deerstalking*, Scrope – or, as he modestly dubbed himself, 'Tortoise' – described his first sight of Bruar Lodge shortly after sunrise:

> Huge, lofty, and in the district of Atholl, second only in magnitude to Ben-y-gloe, Ben Dairg [*sic*], or the red mountain, stands dominant. At the right entrance of the pass, the little white and lonely dwelling ... lies a mere speck beneath it. It consists of two small tenements facing each other, encompassed by a wall, so as to form a small court between them: one of these buildings serves for the master and the other for his servants; there is besides a lodging-place for the hillmen, rather frail in structure, and a dog-kennel of the same picturesque character. Close by stands a stack of peats. Down winds the river Bruar through the glen, sometimes creeping silently through the mossy stones, and at others raving, maddening and bearing all before it, so that neither man nor beast may withstand its violence.

Bruar Lodge today is not quite as Scrope found it, but the approach is very much the same, and its general appearance from a distance with the hills and moorland rising steeply all around.

The immense Atholl forest provided Scrope with an abundance of sport, mainly grouse-shooting and stalking, and appealed strongly to his romantic, artistic temperament. A man of 'highly cultivated taste', as Scott described him, Scrope had been educated at Eton and Oxford, and thereafter at St Luke's Academy in Rome. He was a Fellow of the Linnean Society and was considered by Scott and others to be one of the finest amateur watercolourists of his day. This claim was amply supported by the many illustrations in his books.

From his early twenties, by which time he was already financially independent, Scrope travelled widely throughout Europe. By the time he arrived at Bruar, he was middle-aged, but he was extremely fit and agile and a first-class rifle-shot.

Scrope brought a small armoury of guns and rifles with him to Bruar. His beautiful weapons, some of which are displayed at Blair Castle, were single-shot black-powder muzzle-loaders, of dimensions equivalent to the modern 16-bore shotgun. They performed erratically, throwing a heavy soft-lead bullet which dropped an inch for every twelve feet. In these circumstances, to make certain of killing a stag, Scrope found no alternative but to approach to well within a hundred yards of his target. He carried several rifles, all primed and loaded, and brought a pair of deerhounds with him, ready to be unleashed should he miss or send the deer away lightly wounded. In Scrope's opinion, 'the best dog for chasing deer would unquestionably be the original Scotch or Irish greyhound'. He owned four: Corrie, Tarff, Oscar and 'that eager devil Ossian'. The dogs were the cream of a strain whose colours ranged from yellow to dark-grey, with black ear-tips, eyes and noses.

Except for the use of dogs, the methods practised by Scrope vary surprisingly little from stalking techniques of the present day. The modern high-velocity small-bore rifle has considerably reduced the margins of error. But the approach, across or into the wind, the

patient scanning with the glass (or, as it was termed attractively in Scrope's day, 'the prospect'), the stalk itself whose object is to bring the sportsman as close as possible before firing, all remain nearly identical to the stalking procedures of the early nineteenth century. These well-tried techniques had been adopted all over the Highlands by sportsmen in pre-Victorian times. Scrope was the first man to formulate them, however, and to describe deerstalking as an occupation, although he did not invent the term, which had originated more than a century before, about the time of the 1715 Rebellion.

The first edition of *The Art of Deerstalking* contained 436 discursive pages which were embellished not only with Scrope's own drawings

but also with those of the brothers Charles and Edwin Landseer, whom Scrope knew well, and who added dogs and figures to his keenly observed landscapes. The lithographer, Harding, employed a blue-tint process which Scrope believed 'greatly heightened the aerial perspective' of the plates.

It is true that the overload of literary allusion slows the narrative and would probably aggravate present-day readers, but there is much charm and a vivid sense of reality in Scrope's pithy conversations with his servants and local characters such as the 'Gown-cromb', a blacksmith in a village in Badenoch.

However facetious he might have appeared, Scrope rapidly made friends with the country folk of Atholl, just as he won the admiration and affection of his companions on the hill by his dedication, manly spirit and easy, confiding manner. His good relationships with the Atholl hillmen, Peter Fraser, John and Charlie Crerar and Peter MacLaren, hastened and consolidated his stalking successes and greatly enhanced his delight in the life of the 'high tops'.

In his book Scrope immortalised these men, their prejudices, their dry humour and their language; just as he portrayed them lively, clad in bonnet and kilt, running hard after the deer, or stooping cautiously spying out the far distance from the shelter of a rock.

Much of the initial popularity of *The Art of Deerstalking* was no doubt due to the fact that the Highlands, despite their increasing attraction, were still relatively difficult and expensive to reach; still relatively wild, although far safer and less forbidding than they had been a century before; and for the most part still far beyond communication. (It is worth remembering that Scrope was born the year before Boswell and Johnson began their historic Hebridean tour.) The Highlands retained the irresistible fascination of the mysterious and the lure of the unknown.

Each season from 1822 to 1831 Scrope kept the Duke of Atholl's household, and many friends including Sir Walter Scott, liberally supplied with venison. At the age of sixty, Scrope regretfully abandoned the energetic excitements of the hill for the no less skilled, though physically less demanding, sport of fishing. His only other publication, entitled *Days and Nights of Salmon Fishing*, followed *The Art of Deerstalking* in 1843. The former recounted

Tortoise's experiences on the River Tweed, and like its predecessor, reappeared in various editions. But it was on the high hills and the moors that Scrope attained the peak of his fulfilment, among the deer and the ever-changing light, where the stillness is broken only by the sighing wind or the dash of distant, falling water.

Scrope lived on for twenty years after leaving Bruar, often residing at his fashionable London house in what he called with feeling the 'cheerless glen' of Belgrave Square. But, as he made clear in the grateful dedication to the Duchess of Atholl which prefaced *The Art of Deerstalking*, the most significant period of his life – the years devoted to 'the pleasures of … mountain sport' – had by then already come to an end.

Tramping through Glen Tilt in winter with Beinn a' Ghlo wreathed in mist and the rain lashing down from the north, I have often thought of Scrope's descriptions of witchcraft in Atholl, and in particular the dreaded Witch of Beinn a' Ghlo.

I remember finding a ruined shieling in some flat meadows a few miles north of Tarff on the way to Loch Tilt. The eerie stillness of the place and the pathetic overgrown ruins reminded me of a story Scrope told of the Witch, whose last sighting by mortal men is said to have occurred in 1773.

One stormy night, two poachers came floundering down off the moors in a fierce blizzard. By extraordinary chance, they found a shieling – for all I know, it might have been the same one I'd been looking at – where they were fed and sheltered by a haggard old crone whose hair was lank and whose expression was full of vice and cunning.

In return for her hospitality, the old woman demanded that at midnight, on the first Monday of every month throughout the season, the men must leave a 'fat Hart' or a yeld-hind (a barren animal, unable to give milk) by Fraser's Cairn in Glen Banvie, otherwise, she threatened, 'the ravens shall croak your dirge and your banes shall be picket by the eagle'. Fraser's Cairn, unless there is another by the same name, is set high up on the moors, close to the place where I heard the mysterious bird-calls which receded quite literally from a yard in front of me to fifty yards and more, with the caller never once in view. Perhaps the Witch was also a sort of moorland Rima! But whereas Hudson's bird-girl was shy and benevolent, the Witch of Beinn a' Ghlo was an evil force in the Atholl country, who, it is said, drove cattle into bogs, drowned men and women, destroyed bridges and rode horses half to death.

Caught in wind and sleet, far out on the Glen Tilt moors, it is not difficult to imagine the Witch, perched on her throne of Carn nan Gabhar, at the summit of Beinn a' Ghlo, conducting the mighty orchestra of the storm!

17 August

After breakfast, I helped my father to stack most of the remaining logs and then I went off to my room and made a watercolour sketch of the fishermen from Toulon against a background of Forest Lodge.

In the afternoon, I thought of walking up through Glen Tilt for one last look at Marble Lodge; and then I decided against the idea and instead tramped across the Banvie moor. I jotted down some notes about the weather and colours: 'Mild and dry. Hills a lovely shade of dark blue. The moor a patchwork of brown and purple and sunny green turf'. Nothing very dramatic perhaps, but strange how a few simple phrases keep the memories of good times alive and fresh.

Although it had been many years since I lived there, whenever I walked past Marble Lodge on my way north to Fealar, or Braemar, or Glen Feshie, I always felt a pang of regret, mixed with good feelings, a strange confusion of sad and happy associations which the little house invariably brought to mind. Perhaps this was the reason I chose Glen Banvie instead of Glen Tilt for the last day's tramping of the summer.

The past was not to be disposed of so readily, however. When I got home that evening, rummaging about in some old suitcases in the attic I found a notebook which contained several pages of wildflowers I'd collected from the hills behind Marble Lodge in August 1970.

There was an inscription, written out in the shape of a leaf, which read:

M.M. & A.M.
Wildflowers collected on the
Hill behind Marble Lodge
and along the track and
beside the River
to the south
west of it
on
Monday
August
10th
1970.

When I took a three-year lease of the lodge, the Duke of Atholl's mother, the late Hon Mrs Robert Campbell-Preston, encouraged me to suggest ways and means of improving the living-quarters. These were dark and rather cramped compared to the light, airy rooms at the cottage on Skye where we had spent the previous winter.

Mrs Campbell-Preston, who is sorely missed by everyone who knew her, was one of those people in life who gets things done, someone to whom expressions like 'cannot' and 'problem' mean nothing. The idea of re-planning Marble Lodge appealed to her tremendously. The collection of musty apartments facing the river were opened up as one long sitting-room, with a small panelled bedroom at one end and a kitchen at the other. A new front door with a glass panel brightened the room, which was partly re-floored and painted white; and the estate mason built a fine wide fireplace of rough stone which he topped off with a plank of Scots oak two inches thick.

We had great fun collecting the odds and ends of furniture and crockery we needed. At the Pitlochry saleroom, one Saturday afternoon, we bought a seventy-two-piece Willow Pattern dinner-service for three pounds and a dozen large Kilner jars for half a crown apiece!

Mrs Campbell-Preston gave me the run of a big store room near the castle and generously allowed us to borrow chairs and tables and a fine military chest from the Crimean War which we used for blankets and extra clothing. All these were loaded one morning on to a farm lorry and carried up the glen by the high track. I remember the driver of the lorry pulling up at the crest of the track above the rifle-range, and, gazing at the landscape bathed in sunshine, turned to me and exclaimed, 'These are my mountains! Man, you're fortunate to be coming here.'

In those days, the lodge had no electricity or telephone, neither of which we missed. The oil-lamps were trimmed and lit in the evening and there was a good supply of cut logs in the woodshed. Cooking was done by calor-gas, which was a slow, rather smelly affair. But nobody was in a hurry and the food prepared by this method tasted every bit as delicious as any meal I have tasted since,

coming from a modern, fully equipped kitchen. It all depends who is in charge. Gadgetry makes no difference whatever to the end result.

In the late evening, herds of deer came down to the water's edge to drink, and housemartins had built no fewer than twenty-seven nests round the eaves. One of the keepers suggested that he might knock the nests down with a stick. 'Look at the mess these birds are making,' he said. But we told him very firmly that the pleasure of the housemartins and their young compensated infinitely for the trouble of brushing away a few droppings from the front doorstep, so the nests remained. The keeper's remark angered me at the time, but I realised afterwards that he had only meant to be helpful. Not all keepers are keen naturalists, though I believe it is fair to state that those interested in natural history far outnumber the rest. This man was an exceptionally tidy individual who took a pride in his appearance and the plot of garden by his cottage.

I passed the same cottage the other day. The lawn had been newly mown and the edges neatly trimmed. On the other side of the fence lay a dead sheep, and I thought how strange the countryside sometimes is – a fly-mown lawn and a fly-blown sheep side by side.

Having a too well-manicured garden round the lodge struck me as being rather silly and out of character with the surroundings. But the grass and shrubs never really got out of hand; and, besides, it was good to see daffodils and nasturtiums growing up wild among the grass, and the scattering of bluebells which appeared in springtime.

There was so much to do that first August that I kept very little in the way of records. But the notebook with the wildflowers pressed into it has a short description of one very special day when the glen was still quite new to me. I'd worked hard all morning getting the house straight, washing floors and arranging the heavier pieces of furniture. After lunch, I climbed the hill behind Marble Lodge and found a big mossy stone set at a slant, leaning back into the face of the hill. I lay down with my back to the boulder and drank up the scenery, which that day was well-nigh perfect. I wrote:

It is all so wonderfully peaceful here above the river. The far bank levels back for a short distance and then rises steeply to a soft green ridge. Along the river bank a mixture of hawthorn, oak and rowan and little ragged stands of birch are growing down the hillside. There is a dark concentration of green stuff and gnarled limbs overhanging the dark brown fishy water from which comes no reflection or sparkle; only a hoarse, rushing sound as if the river were out of breath.... The slopes to the north are white with sheep. To the south they are thickly forested with spruce and larches which, from a distance, gives them a hazy appearance, as if they were just out of focus.

The sunshine encloses me with a comfortable, all enfolding warmth – a gloriously alive, vibrant feeling – which binds me closer to the earth and makes every atom of my body glad to be in contact with the grass and the infinite depth of earth and rock below. I am suspended in the realm of ideal contentment, like a diver far below the sea's surface. The light is strange and luminous like the sea light. All around me are open-hearted yellow buttercups with their delicate, convex, glossy petals clustered about a core of palest green. These and the sharp spiny thistles are my companions on the hill today; each of us is given up entirely – like hedonists – to the wide blue sky and the sun. The housemartins swim like fishes in the calm, blue atmosphere, calling to each other – 'Pee-eet ... pee-eet'.

When I go down this evening and read *Idle Days in Patagonia* by the lamplight after supper, I shall find a new meaning in Hudson's beautiful descriptions of starlight on the pampas and flocks of purple swallows, and the delicate faint perfume of the evening primrose ...

There are two sides to every coin, of course. In contrast to the mild spring and summer weather, winters in Glen Tilt were frequently severe. In January the temperature at Marble Lodge dropped as low as minus 25 degrees, and it was essential to drain the tanks and shut off the water supply during the months when the house was uninhabited.

In spite of being so remote – or perhaps because of this – neither the lodge nor its contents were ever tampered with except once, when a hill-walker, caught in a storm late in the evening, broke a window, let himself in and spent the night. One of the keepers, who noticed the broken pane on his way by, brought our keys from the Estate Office and searched the house. Nothing had been touched, however; and the keeper found a message scribbled on an envelope, apologising for the damage and enclosing a pound note with which to repair the broken window!

He said we'd been lucky on this occasion, but I prefer to think that anyone who loves the hills enough to tramp them in the dead of winter might have done the same.

A hard winter claims many victims among the deer, in particular the older stags, exhausted by the rut and starved of grazing by the deep, frozen snow.

In February 1985 I happened to be in Glen Banvie, some miles to the west of Marble Lodge and the Tilt, watching a herd of 140 stags strung out across the moor not far from the confluence of the Allt an t-Seapail burn and the Allt na Moine Baine.

The stags were plunging shoulder-deep through the snowbound heather, feeding in small groups towards higher ground. Some, which had been feeding among the lighter covering of snow near the river, crossed the indented, bluish-white ribbon of track and vanished behind the low hummocks before reappearing further up. I saw several bound forward eagerly, their necks held stiffly erect, as the going got firmer, and then crash, floundering in the soft drifts which masked the channels made by tiny burns draining down off the hillside.

Other stags had slumped down on their haunches near the crest, weary of scraping for food, basking in a glimpse of cold sunshine. The leaders halted at the skyline, watching their companions' ungainly progress. Some way beyond, a widely scattered herd of about seventy beasts had spread out across the gently rising ground above the confluence of the two burns.

About 500 yards away, between the track and the river, three stags lingered far behind the main herd, two of them feeding restlessly in circles, a third standing stock-still, head up, facing straight away from me. Something about the attitudes and behaviour of this little group looked odd and held my attention.

Presently, the stag nearest the track broke away and cantered uphill, out of sight. The others stayed exactly as they were, one motionless, the other moving restlessly to and fro between it and the brow of the river bank. After a while, the stag which had been feeding approached its companion and began nuzzling its cheek. This procedure was repeated twice more with emphasis. There was a long pause. Then this stag too wheeled away at a slow canter, until it finally caught up with the stragglers beyond the line of hillocks. The stag left alone beside the water stood quite unmoved, staring fixedly in the direction of the confluence and the arc of deer grazing unconcernedly above it.

I left my vantage-point, overcome by curiosity, and walked very slowly down the track towards the solitary stag. My movements alarmed the deer on the nearby slopes, which immediately closed ranks, and in the distance I could see several of the smaller herd, also alerted, watching me. The stag's antlers swayed like the branches of a tree stirred by the breeze. I saw through the glasses that he had been a ten-pointer, but one of the cup-tines had been broken. As I moved gradually closer, his whole body seemed to sway; and, at fifty yards, his head jerked suddenly backwards and he collapsed on his haunches, rolling heavily on his right side.

The stag lashed out with his upper front and back legs in powerful, convulsive jerks as he struggled vainly to rise. I hurried forward, anxious to discover the cause, but at the same time keeping well behind him, in an effort not to frighten the stricken animal. The effort was wasted, of course, for by then he had seen me. He dragged himself round in a half-circle to face the river and lay with his shaggy neck outstretched, his legs drawn up under him, eyes bloodshot, his nostrils quivering and dilating as he fought for breath. Spattered in the bruised snow at his belly were some tiny specks of blood, the colour of wild clover.

I waited quietly beside him as the remnants of his strength, sapped by age, the autumn rut and the intense cold, faded. The gleam of life in his eye faded slowly, as the light fades from a spent filament of electric wire. He died there, while the wind ruffled the plumes of his grey and russet coat.

The stags, massed at the ridge above me, gazed down on him, except for a handful which continued pawing and scraping for food amongst the frozen snow. The seventy deer fanned out above the confluence of the Seapail and the Moine Baine also stood watching attentively like cattle, silent witnesses of the fallen beast's last moments of distress.

When I looked up again, a few moments later, the deer had vanished like smoke. They left an eerie sensation, one of emptiness, which remained with me throughout the long walk back to the lodge.

The keeper in Glen Banvie told me that during the 1984–5 winter, eighty stags had been found dead in various parts of the forest. He added that the experience of seeing a stag drop dead from natural causes was uncommon. My story moved him, I think, as much as I had been moved; more so perhaps because he was better able to appreciate the circumstances. The keeper had shot a large number of stags in his day, and had been in at the death of many more, but he was a good naturalist, keenly interested in the life of the moor, and his heart had not been hardened by the years of culling and stalking deer for sport.

I believe the same holds true for most sportsmen and sportswomen. As a boy, my family encouraged my interest in natural history, but they never attempted to suppress my youthful passion for shooting which, I daresay, seems an odd contradiction. Wisely, they left me to work out for myself any dilemma which might have existed.

I am inclined to think that much of the excitement derived from matters not directly involved with the act of killing game. I loved the smell of gun-oil and the acrid stench of burnt cordite; the feel of a well-made gun or rifle and the satisfaction of a successful approach, pitting one's wits against the infinitely sharper wits of the quarry. The business of pulling the trigger often came as an anticlimax. I cannot deny the thrill, but the sight of the dead animal or bird always vaguely troubled me and over the years my enthusiasm for field sports gradually waned.

In the Highlands, culling deer is necessary for their survival. The same applies to wildlife management in Africa and elsewhere. Shooting for sport, hard though it may be to accept the fact, is also a vital part of conservation. And of course, when all is said and done, the greater truth remains that 'each man kills the thing he loves'.

I tried as far as possible to avoid too much sentiment when writing the tale of the dying stag. A century ago, in Victorian times, an excess of sentiment and romance would have mattered less to the general reader. But modern generations view the relationship between man and animals differently. The gooey mixture of romance and anthropomorphism is nowadays as unpopular as it was lapped up by Landseer's admirers. And for my part I believe in the modern view, although I cannot deny the thrill I experience whenever I see a fine, original example of Landseer's painting.

As a young man, Edwin Landseer visited Bruar Lodge in 1826, while Scrope was still the shooting-tenant. As a result of his visit, Landseer became passionately devoted to deer-stalking and for a long period he returned every year to the Highlands, mainly to Glen Feshie where the Duchess of Bedford had built a wild, romantic encampment which epitomised Queen Victoria's dream of 'wilderness, liberty and solitude'.

Here, Landseer stalked and painted the great stags as they moved like the drift of light and shadow among the dying colours of the Highland year. It has been said that Landseer's success stemmed from his ability to identify both with the stalker and his quarry, and this is undoubtedly true. Although Landseer was an energetic, wiry little man, conversely many of his paintings turned out large and drenched in excessive sentimentality. He never learned to shoot well despite years of practice, and often, to the consternation of the ghillies, at the climax of a long approach Landseer's artistic curiosity

overcame his sporting instinct and he would settle down to sketch a stag instead of killing it.

What has been called 'the distinctive, anthropomorphic heroism' implicit in Landseer's work – which Victorians adored – has been dismissed as frivolous and reprehensible by later generations. Certainly 'The Monarch of the Glen', superbly crowned with beautifully symmetrical antlers of a mighty girth and spread, might have been Marlborough after Blenheim or Wellington after Waterloo. The head stalker at Black Mount in Argyllshire once remarked to me that in his opinion the Monarch was much too heavy-bodied for a typical Highland stag – a good one at that.

Landseer's dying stags all too often glanced dramatically away like some heroine of the Victorian stage at the point of death by poison, the folds of her dress decorously arranged on a *chaise-longue*. Attitudes like these, however appealing to a mass audience, detracted from Landseer's acutely observed and wonderfully rendered animal studies, which in my own humble view have never been surpassed.

But there was little or no 'distancing' of the artist from his subjects. Magnificent as they are, compositions such as 'The Fatal Duel' and the famous 'Stag at Bay' displayed too much humanity, and in spite of their superb accuracy, too much romantic pose. Perhaps this had something to do with Landseer's treatment of eyes. They had a human rather than animal quality. One imagines his stags, like old men in a club, scanning the pages of *Country Life* or the *Illustrated London News*. Neither the tame hinds I observed at close range in Glen Tilt and Fealar nor the dying stag that winter near the Banvie burn looked remotely like that, whatever I may have felt at the time.

Landseer's animals lacked the bright unrepining gaze of the wild; of a life founded upon instinct, restless vitality and the struggle to survive. Instead he offered the promise of communication in human terms, which, knowing this to be impossible, people nowadays resent.

From boyhood, I have taken a great interest in the artist–naturalists who painted the wildlife of the Highlands: men like John Guille Millais, who was a boy of eight when Landseer died in 1873.

Millais's art was influenced by his father to an extent, the great

Pre-Raphaelite painter Sir J.E. Millais; just as he studied and respected the work of Landseer and other outstanding animal-painters of the day, notably Joseph Wolf. John Millais, as a boy of twelve, tramped the length of the Scottish east coast, shooting and sketching wildfowl which he skinned and mounted. Unlike Landseer, Millais grew up a dedicated and highly proficient naturalist and sportsman, a fine shot and a tireless collector of hunting trophies. A folio volume, *British Deer and their Horns*, printed in 1897 and illustrated with Millais's drawings and paintings, contained a few pictures reminiscent of Landseer; one, for example, entitled 'They Kill us for their Sport', which depicts a dead stag slumped among the rocks beside a cascade of foaming water, while an eagle, its wings uplifted, soars above the corpse against a curtain of swirling mist.

Yet here the similarity ceases. Millais's stag was a lifeless animal, no more and no less. Nowhere in his painting did Millais ever attempt to bridge the gulf which separates animal and human understanding. *British Deer and their Horns* is not merely beautiful to look at, but it has made a profound contribution to scientific knowledge of the species of native and imported deer found in this country. As a draughtsman Millais excelled, and his many attitude drawings, for instance 'Stags Feeding as they Move' or 'Wild Stags – August', captured the spirit and action of Highland red deer with a degree of perfection which, to my mind, has never been equalled. Millais's popularity has continued to this day and the warmth and humour of his work, which so appeals to sportsmen and lovers of wild nature in every generation, sets it apart, in my opinion, even from the magnificent achievements of his friend and contemporary, Archibald Thorburn.

There have been several other fine painters of deer, the most outstanding among them perhaps being V.R. Balfour-Browne, whose watercolours I remember gloating over at Black Mount; Lionel Edwards, better known for his paintings of horses and huntsmen; and Frank Wallace, whom I had the privilege of meeting, a close friend of J.G. Millais and Lionel Edwards and a fine exponent of pen-and-ink and pencil drawing.

Harold Frank Wallace was born in 1881 and inherited a considerable artistic talent from his mother's family. From an early age he became imbued with a love of animals, and deer in particular. Frank Wallace's early paintings, following a period of tuition at the famous Calderón School in London, testified to the influence of Millais and Thorburn. He met Millais in 1897 when he was sixteen; and later, in the 1920s, he became a friend of the Calderón School's star pupil, Lionel Edwards. Wallace and Edwards painted frequently in each other's company. Until then, Wallace had been – as young people say nowadays – rather 'laid back' in his approach. But he was encouraged by Lionel Edwards's hardworking, tirelessly critical example, and from then until about 1939 Wallace's painting improved and grew markedly freer, as step by step he gained confidence and found his own means of expressing the Highland scene.

I have heard various experts, gallery owners among them, say that Wallace painted deer more accurately than Millais or another much sought-after artist, George Lodge; but surely such observations are pointless. When you stop to consider the wealth of talent possessed by all these men, there can be no question of setting one off against another. This is an attitude they themselves would have despised. Whether you are drawn to Millais, Wallace, Edwards or Balfour-Browne is all a matter of personal taste.

Many of the artists I have mentioned were also excellent writers, and Frank Wallace was no exception. He wrote a number of interesting, highly entertaining books about his hunting experiences in China, New Zealand and Australia, as well as Scotland, and for many years he contributed regular articles to magazines such as *The Field* and *Country Life*. During the Second World War, he was appointed Deer Controller of Scotland. He lived and worked mainly on a beautiful estate, Corrimony, in Glen Urquhart which overlooks Ben Wyvis, one of his favourite hills. A small private exhibition held in London in 1920 confirmed Wallace's notable gift for composition and his unerring eye for detail. A reviewer, writing in *Country Life*, stressed that 'Mr Wallace possesses the rare ability of being able to present real deer in real scenery', and added perceptively that the deer which Wallace painted never mastered their surroundings, nor were they overshadowed by them.

This was a supreme compliment paid to one of the finest exponents of the modern school of sporting art. It is a gift rarely seen, and I can think of only three artists painting at the present time whose work reflects it in the same degree: Rodger McPhail, and Brian Rawling with whom I have had the somewhat undeserved honour of sharing several exhibitions in Scotland during the past six or seven years; and, of course, Raoul Millais, John Guille Millais's younger son, who was also Thorburn's godson.

Heaven forbid that I should give the impression of setting my own work on a par with these first-rate men. But the years of tramping and sketching among the hills, and the hundreds of hours spent observing deer, if nothing else have helped me to appreciate something of the skill and patience which sets their paintings far above the rest.

18 August

A dry and cloudy start. I was up this morning at 6.50 a.m. getting my few belongings packed, ready for a journey to Argyllshire.

Someone remarked at breakfast: 'You'll be sorry to leave.' And so I was, for the summer in Perthshire had been splendid. True enough, the weather might have been kinder. This had made no difference to the days spent tramping, but it did mean that many of my sketches had to be finished indoors, which was a pity, but not the end of the world.

'Now for the worthless statistics', I scribbled in my diary. Totting up mileages is a bit like judging a good dinner by the size of the bill. For what it's worth, I found that I had tramped not quite 450 miles in forty days and filled two thick notebooks and made something like fifty-five sketches. The old haversack which accompanied me all the way had been one which my father carried into Normandy on D-Day Plus Two – 8 June 1944. My father happened to mention this fact while I was packing and I saw him examine the numbers stencilled on the right shoulder-strap: 20-4-W-40-459. My father is a man of few words. He has told me very little about his days fighting in the War and very little about the landing, apart from the weather during the Channel crossing, which was pretty rough. And he grinned: 'Fancy, remembering that I was sea-sick!' I have a strong suspicion that he did not care to think too much about what happened afterwards. I have had very little experience of rough seas, but a few months ago, when my wife and I were travelling by hovercraft from Dover to Boulogne in a Force 6 gale, the vessel became airborne for a few seconds before it struck the trough of a twelve-foot wave, which put my father's remark into perspective.

One of the most famous deer forests in the West is Black Mount in Argyllshire. On my last visit, I travelled from Blair Atholl through Glen Lyon to Crianlarich, and from there to Bridge of Orchy.

Thanks to a kind invitation, I was housed at Forest Lodge, which is situated at the south end of the drove-road, overlooking Loch Tulla and the main house. The only other occupant of the lodge was an elderly water-bailiff who divided the year between Black Mount and his native Benbecula, off the west coast. The water-bailiff was hospitable and informative and the three or four days I spent there were thoroughly enjoyable – not least on account of the weather, which had improved dramatically so that we woke every morning to sunshine and clear blue skies.

Black Mount was made famous by Lady Breadalbane, who in 1907 wrote a book entitled *The High Tops of Black Mount*, filled with evocative descriptions of the hill and, of course, deer-stalking which she loved. Lady Breadalbane must have been an extraordinary woman. She was someone to be reckoned with, a personality not easily forgotten or ignored who combined forcefulness and charm.

She clambered about the hills in a tweed jacket cut in the Edwardian fashion and a long tweed skirt which came down to her ankles. Her dress was probably quite practical in its way, combining propriety with some protection from horseflies, which the stalkers refer to as 'clegs', and the furiously biting midges. By all accounts Lady Breadalbane was a fine shot with a rifle, although her performances, I fancy, were eclipsed by the present laird's mother, who, at the time of her death had killed no less than 800 stags!

As much as Lady Breadalbane's writing, I have always enjoyed looking at the photographs which illustrate *The High Tops of Black Mount*, which make up for their rather indifferent quality by giving a true and very interesting picture of Highland sport as it was at the turn of the century.

After supper on my first evening, Hector, the head stalker, took
me out in his Landrover to look for deer. The sky was cloudless, the
air warm and still. A few miles along the drove-road leading to
Glencoe, Hector stopped the truck, got out and pointed across a
stretch of moorland to where he had noticed five hinds feeding.
Handing me his brass-bound three-draw telescope he advised me to
sight above it first, holding the telescope as I would a rifle and then,
having pinpointed the target, squint through the eye-piece.

'There's really nothing to it,' said Hector. But I found that using a telescope was far more difficult than I'd imagined, owing to its high magnification which tended to exaggerate the trembling of one's hands, and its narrow field of vision. After a good many failures, I managed to pick up two of the hinds which, as I adjusted the focus, flashed immediately closer, sharp and clear in the bright disc of the lens.

By trial and error I slowly got accustomed to using the telescope and one by one found the other three hinds. For a while we lay on our backs in the long grass watching them – Hector peering intently through his binoculars – until the midges drove us back to the shelter of the truck.

Hector's eyesight was amazing. At dusk he pointed out two more hinds, silhouetted on a ridge, well over a thousand yards away. 'Look, now,' he cautioned, 'there's one facing us. See her? Just above the other and a wee bit to the left.' I located the hinds finally, with the help of Hector's binoculars, standing exactly as he'd described them.

So it went on throughout the evening. He assured me that much of it came with practice and experience, knowing what to look for. He had spent most of his life on the hill and I have no doubt whatever that what he said is correct.

On the way back, Hector gave me careful instructions about how best to approach the ridge. He advised me to strike out from about the same spot where we had lain near the drove-road watching the small herd of hinds, and follow the course of a burn across the steeply rising moor. There I would find a cliff about forty feet high running diagonally across the face of the hill. The way continued along the base of this cliff, aiming for the west, between it and another shallower escarpment. A stiff climb would bring me up to the ridge. He warned that I must keep a sharp lookout for the stags which frequented this ground. In their late-summer coats, camouflaged by the grass and stones and the restless light, they were difficult to spot except by a practised eye. Hector had no need to emphasise this last word of advice. The first evening had proved that.

Next morning the sun came out from behind a big drift of white cloud as I lay on a grassy incline screened by boulders. The approach to the ridge had not worked out as planned. Hector's route depended on a steady south-south-west wind. Unfortunately the morning found the wind direction changed to north-north-east, which meant that the whole procedure had to be reversed. This brought me out well below the ridge, which gave the stags a better chance of seeing me. As it turned out, I was lucky, and managed to crawl to within 300 yards of a herd of forty stags, grazing uphill across a scarred rock-face which the sunlight here threw into sharp relief.

The sun glinted on their horns and their coats which were variously coloured, as usual, from oatmeal to dark tawny brown. They were beautiful to watch as they stole forward a pace at a time up the rocky hillside, facing into the wind.

The vast shadow of a cloud passed over the wide sweep of the glen, over the distant peaks and corries towards Glen Etive and the sea. Larks rose in twos and threes from the warm upland grass. Meadow-pipits darted from rock to rock. Some of the stags sank down among the lichen-encrusted rocks, relaxed and contented in the warm morning air. The sun dried out the coarse grasses, blade by blade, and the bitter scent of grass and heather filled my nostrils as I rested on my elbows, following the movements of the herd through the glasses.

The last stag in the scattered line was an old gaunt fellow with a pale, mangy coat. His antlers were curved like an enormous wish-bone. I counted five points each side, a long gap between the brow-tine and the cup, a sure indication of age. He moved slowly, as though he suffered from rheumatism, and stopped every few yards to paw the ground and graze. Now and again he flicked his ears to brush away the flies. Sometimes he lifted his head and stood there, gazing.

The wind blew steadily from the north-east across the face of the hill. A true wind that left nothing for me to do except to lie quiet, out of sight.

The herd settled to feed on a sloping terrace. The old ten-pointer, who had been trailing them, suddenly advanced towards a young beast which was resting, partly hidden by a boulder. The young stag remained where he was, ignoring his elder who tossed his head violently as though giving a command. The young stag got up and stood with his back to the other. The old beast thereupon lifted a fore-foot and kicked the young one deliberately on the behind! The young stag walked on a pace or two and then lowered his head to graze. The ten-pointer followed and kicked him again, a much harder blow this time, which apparently had the desired effect. The young stag cantered uphill, the older beast following, to the summit of a grassy strip, where it lay down on a little hummock, keeping watch while the old stag began to graze peacefully a short distance away, now confident of the other's protection.

Fifty yards further down the terrace, a beautiful stag with fine thick horns stood poised on some rocks like a perfect replica of Landseer's 'Monarch'. This animal was lighter-bodied, however, and to my mind more attractive in consequence. He had a bright russet-gold coat and appeared wonderfully agile and alive.

I continued to watch the stags for an hour until for no good reason (or so I thought) those farthest up the incline began to move rapidly towards the summit followed by the rest, who galloped after the leaders, taking the ziggurat-steps of boulder-strewn turf in their stride, until the last of them had disappeared. What had caused them to move so suddenly I couldn't guess until a hiking couple, dressed in bright-yellow nylon jerkins, marched unconcernedly into full view, making for Stob a Choire Odhair. A polite, cheery pair, they grasped the situation at once and apologised, adding that in the stalking season they always made a point of calling at the stalker's cottage before going onto the hills, so as to be certain which direction they might safely take. This simple courtesy causes hill-walkers no inconvenience and leaves the estate owner and his guests to enjoy their sport undisturbed.

The hikers tramped off in the opposite direction to the stags and I waited for the length of time it took to smoke a cigarette before attempting to follow the herd. The ascent which the fleeing stags had made so gracefully and effortlessly turned out to be far steeper than it looked, and I arrived at the top panting and out of breath, having flushed out a big dog-fox on the way. The summit reached at last, I threw myself down to get my second wind and scanned the ground for the stags. Eventually I found them: tiny flecks of red and white, feeding away from me in a huge green basin a thousand feet below.

The day after, I tried to locate the herd without success – in fact, I saw no deer at all – wandering in Coireach a Ba and the mysteriously beautiful Coirean Easain whose deeply riven flanks the sunlight flattened like a photograph. The strange, two-dimensional unreality of these hills left a strong impression on my mind. There was an irresistible pleasure in these wild places. The fact that I didn't find the stag herd seemed unimportant by comparison.

Returning along the boggy floor of Coireach a Ba, a pair of greenshanks circled me for a while, diving down in a series of mock attacks. Their tuneful whistle, floating in the wind, symbolised the solitude.

How right the intrepid Lady Breadalbane was, for the charm and the uncompromising wildness of Black Mount lies in its hills and misty corries, its ever-changing patterns of light and the herds of wild Red deer.

The water-bailiff who lived at Forest Lodge was an archetypal Scotsman of the knobbly-kneed 'Och aye the noo' variety. He talked incessantly and was very partial to a 'dram'; but he was exceedingly knowledgeable too, and a harmless, good-natured, kind-hearted soul whose company I enjoyed.

Hector was a different character entirely. No less kindly or hospitable, like the stalkers of olden days deer were his overriding passion. He was tubby, but do not be deceived, Hector could walk the hind legs off a donkey, as they say, and even although he admitted to smoking fifty or sixty cigarettes a day, on the hill he climbed and scrambled with the best of them and seemed to have as much high-grade oxygen in his lungs as a hot-air balloon. Compared to his neighbour the water-bailiff, Hector was a temperate man; a pot of his wife's good strong tea was his favourite beverage. I have only met two estate-stalkers who were strict teetotallers, and if anything Hector was the stricter of the two. He was a mine of information, and his knowledge of deer and their habits was literally encyclopaedic. When I came to write up my adventures at Black Mount, I said, 'They are each fine, old-fashioned characters in their way. Hector is a great stalker and the water-bailiff, bless his heart, is a great talker.' I ought to have added, 'And no offence meant', but I assumed that would be taken for granted....

The two or three evenings I spent with Hector and his family, when my host at Forest Lodge was engaged on other business, were memorable and a delight. Hector's wife baked scones and made jam the like of which, if they appeared in Fortnum & Mason, would cause a riot. Hector's family would sit quietly by while he spoke of days he remembered on the hill. He seldom spoke of 'red-letter' days, now that I think of it, but mostly about what he had seen and the simple, uneventful things which happen to us all along the way, the great difference being that Hector could read the landscape like an open book – the book of Nature, which, for him, had no beginning and no end.

His knowledge of stalking literature was astounding. He had a fine, small collection of his own, the rarer items such as Scrope's

first edition and the first imprints of St John and Horatio Ross being the only ones missing. But, he said in his quiet way, 'the gentlemen sometimes lend me theirs'. These books, which nowadays cost several hundred pounds each, when you can get them, were doubtlessly read from cover to cover and returned to their owners as tight and unblemished as they were first handed over.

It was Hector who told me that Landseer's 'Monarch' was a fine painting, but that the stag was too well fleshed-out for a good Highland example. He looked through my sketchbooks and made suggestions for improving the accuracy of the drawing – always in a gentle manner, as though he had no right to criticise my work. Hector will never know the extent of my gratitude. A small oil sketch I sent him, which showed the influence of Raoul Millais's instruction, was small thanks for the wealth of information he imparted.

September

The traveller making his way to the Mull of Kintyre from the north passes along a stretch of windswept country, level and productive, at the edge of which the long Atlantic swell breaks white even in calm weather. On the grey autumn day when I wandered south along this beautiful coast-line I could see Islay and Jura on the horizon to the west. There was a deep blueness on those island hills, and heavy shade was on them except for one small pool of golden sunshine on the heathery coast of Jura.... It was a delight to me, coming from the garden-less district of northern Skye, to find that the people of Kintyre had so great a love of flowers. Within a stone's throw of some of these cottage gardens creamy seas broke lazily upon the low sandy shore, where oyster catchers were feeding and bathing, and lapwings were circling in great flocks overhead. Here was the Spirit of Ocean – of the open unbridled Atlantic ...

Thus Seton Gordon described the Kintyre coast in 1935, in his book *Highways and Byways in the West Highlands*, which today remains a *vade mecum* for every traveller in these parts of Scotland. Seton Gordon's word-picture of autumn in the south-west could scarcely be bettered; and his book's illustrator, Sir D.Y. Cameron RA, gave a charming sketch of 'Atlantic Waves, Kintyre', which showed the lowering grey sky and showering spray at the point where land and sea collide.

I had hoped that it would be possible to return there in the spring of 1987 with my uncle, John Templeman, my mother's older brother, who loved Kintyre and the people of Campbeltown. Uncle John's dream was to live there, for all his seventy years spent on the Clyde; but, alas, the dream remained a dream. What was sadder still, he died a month before the journey we had planned was to begin. We had meant to travel about by car. My uncle had suffered a heart attack, followed by angina, and was no longer able to walk as he had liked to walk, for miles, at his own even pace, taking in everything he saw and heard, stopping here and there for a few words with some passer-by. He had loved to bathe in the sea and afterwards lie on the long stretches of deserted beach at Southend, near Campbeltown.

The year before he died, Uncle John wrote a description of Kintyre in a notebook which he called simply, *Reflections*. The notebook contained scraps of poetry, thoughts about his wife whom he adored, about religion and his war years at Scapa Flow. These notes were never intended for publication, but when he gave them to me to read, he told me, 'Keep them, and use them however you please.' The notes described my uncle's visits to Campbeltown with Aunt Cathie, shortly after they were married.

> The first time I went to Campbeltown was with Cathie, by bus. The next visit we made by the steamer, from Fairlie; and after that we went there every year by car.
>
> The journey by car is a very pleasant one, crossing the Clyde by Erskine Bridge to Dumbarton, and then on to Loch Lomond side. The road winds its way past Luss and Tarbet, after that Arrochar with a long climb up the Rest-and-be-Thankful hill.... It is a lovely run, overlooking Jura and its

famous 'Paps' – as the island's breast-shaped hills are known …

Further south John and Cathie came to Bellochantuy, a few miles to the north of Machrihanish on the west coast, where Cathie had gone to the village school and where her family lived until she was twelve.

Cathie's father had worked on a small farm at Lagelgarve, near Bellochantuy, for sixteen years. Her mother milked twelve cows night and morning, working side-by-side with her husband, and her wages were two shillings and sixpence a week – roughly fourpence a day. The farm had been owned by a brother and sister who were getting on in years. They promised that Cathie's father should have the farm after they were gone, but nothing was put down in writing; as a result, another brother from South Africa claimed the farm and Cathie's father was left with nothing to prove the promises they had made …

Perhaps it was for this reason that my aunt refused to go back to live at Campbeltown.

My uncle told me several good stories about Kintyre and several more about our own village, here on the south shore of the River Clyde. One of his favourites concerned Davaar Island, near Campbeltown, off the east coast of Kintyre. In 1884 a local artist named Archibald MacKinnon had a strange dream, or, some say, a vision, of Christ on the cross surrounded by a collection of allegorical figures who represented the sins of the world. While the dream was still vivid in his mind, MacKinnon crossed to Davaar Island by the causeway and painted a picture of Christ on the wall of one of the island's caves. For a time MacKinnon kept his vision and the cave-painting a closely guarded secret. Uncle John told me that, a few months after the painting was finished, some fishermen caught in a storm one night came with lanterns to shelter in the cave. When they saw the life-size figure of Christ appearing out of the gloom, the fishermen nearly died of fright.

MacKinnon's painting deteriorated over the years in the dampness, exposed to the salty sea air. When he was eighty-four, fifty years after he had painted the crucifixion scene, MacKinnon returned once more to Davaar Island and restored the picture, which remains there to this day. I have never seen the painting, except a reproduction made on a local postcard printed by one of Aunt Cathie's relatives in 1934. My uncle said that the painting, seen in its natural setting of the Davaar cave, was impressive and very moving. I do not doubt this for a moment. But it is the combination of location and subject which is striking, rather than the painting itself which seemed to me a lifeless, uninspiring affair composed of rather poorly painted Pre-Raphaelite clichés.

Keeping to the religious theme, Uncle John told me a story about a church minister, the Reverend MacFarlane, who had the reputation of being far and away the politest man in the neighbour-hood. The Reverend MacFarlane invariably raised his hat to every-one he met, parishioners and visitors alike, sometimes three or four times in quick succession when the streets were busy on market day.

One day he was in the middle of a driving test which was going fairly smoothly until one of the Reverend's congregation appeared, whereupon the Reverend raised his hat as usual, taking his hands off the steering wheel, and all three – car, test inspector and minister – landed in the ditch!

A strange, attractive old reprobate in the village where I grew up, who had been a kind of journeyman–tramp, according to Uncle John had fathered children all over the place, including a good many in the village itself. He used to pass a certain shopkeeper standing at his door and call out in a loud voice so that everyone could hear: 'All the very best to your good self and my family!'

The tramp got his come-uppance, however, when one evening the eldest son of his latest conquest came back to their cottage, earlier than expected, and found the tramp and his mother locked in the bedroom. The lad was furious, and threw the tramp's trousers which had been lying on a chair into the fire. The tramp went out of circulation for some time after, until, I imagine, he had managed to beg, borrow or steal another pair of trousers.

This dreadful old creature sometimes appeared in our kitchen in winter – as he used to say, 'just for a heat'. Once he told my grandmother how he had been sitting one evening by the open range in a cottage where he sometimes took lodgings. In spite of his wild ways, the old tramp made a great show of morals and strict Christian principles, which fooled nobody but led my grandmother to suspect that he might not be, after all, quite so bad as he was painted.

Be that as it may, the old man told how the daughter of the house, who was in her late twenties, came into the room where he was sitting and proceeded to undress and change her clothes in front of the fire. The tramp said: 'The shameless hussy stripped herself naked – I tell you, not a stitch of clothing left on her – and then she dressed herself again and flounced out, without speaking a word.'

'But surely you didn't look?' said my grandmother, who was more amused than shocked by the tramp's confession.

'Ach, missus,' he replied, 'the lassie was standing there right in front of me! What else *could* I do but look?'

December

It rained for much of the time during a brief visit I made to Blair Atholl after staying with my uncle at Erskine Cottage.

The fields all round had lines of split turnips laid down for the sheep. Sheep and cattle standing about dripping wet in the dark muddy fields looked thoroughly miserable, dirty and bedraggled. The hard winter covers had closed on the tale of what had been for me a perfect summer. The estate roads were slimed with mud, and smoke from the wood-fires hung like plumes of grey mist over the rooftops in the village. Layers of cloud turned the high ground into a flat table-land and the hills stretched away like black shadows in the gloaming. Every surface – tree-bark, stones and grass – was wet to the touch. But the sharp wind gusting down from the glens brought with it the familiar odour of pine, fresh and tingling, which mingled with the pungent, abrasive scent of burning fire-wood.

A pheasant-shoot had been arranged for Boxing Day and I went along purely as a spectator. For once the weather was kind. I stood in a field near the arboretum beside a couple in green oilskin jackets with a black labrador at their feet. Volley upon volley of shots echoed from the spinney, the dull thud of twelve-bore guns facing away and the sharper bang of others aimed in our direction. Quick flurries of echoes responded to each shot – 'Wha- wha- wha' and 'What-what-what' – as though the landscape demanded an explanation of this unwarranted disturbance.

A cock-pheasant rocketed up over the pines and suddenly folded, beak first, as the bang of the shot reached my ears. Some of the birds rose and fell in a great rainbow arc, while others which had been struck too far back, or had had a wing broken by a pellet, braked sharply in mid-air and fluttered to the ground where they were retrieved by the waiting fleet of soft-mouthed spaniels. There was very little wind that day, and the pheasants' speed had been much reduced. Most of them were killed while flying low over the trees.

The shoot was a tame affair compared to one I attended many years ago in the south-west, near the sea. There, the birds came streaking down with the full blast of an Atlantic wind behind them, travelling well in excess of sixty miles an hour. This sort of shooting divides the men from the boys and makes an exciting day for those who enjoy the sport of driven birds. But the calmer business, like this Christmas shoot, for me savoured too much of target-practice, the guns all keen to 'do well' and the birds falling like autumn leaves, almost faster than they rose.

Everyone – with the possible exception of the pheasants – had a fine day which ended as it had begun in a wintry blue haze, with a clear sky and streamers of white cloud that floated weightlessly before the massed banks of grey in the far west.

On my way home through the Whim Wood, I saw a buzzard lifting slowly off the side of a gully above the burn. The bird needed some effort to become airborne, but after that glided away, its flight appearing like a series of moving-picture frames as it passed behind the line of black tree trunks in a flicker of tawny-brown and white.

A few hundred yards further down the track, an open Land Rover with the day's bag of pheasants heaped up in the back rattled past and stopped just ahead of me. The young keeper leaned out of the window, shook hands and wished me a belated Merry Christmas.

'You'll be away south again after the holiday?' he enquired.

I nodded. 'Yes, I'm afraid so. This weekend.'

'You don't know how lucky you are,' he said, shaking his head wistfully. 'London is a great place. All these picture-houses and bars and discotheques. Something different to do every night, if you want to. Give me the West End and the bright lights! Round about here it's dead in the winter.'

'The trouble is,' I replied, 'there aren't any mountains in Mayfair.'

The young keeper slammed his Land Rover into gear. 'Swap you any day,' he grinned. But, in his heart, I know that he did not really mean it.